EXCELLENCE
BEYOND
COMPLIANCE

ENHANCING ANIMAL WELFARE THROUGH THE
CONSTRUCTIVE USE OF THE ANIMAL WELFARE ACT

EXCELLENCE
BEYOND
COMPLIANCE

"Jim Gesualdi is a knowledgeable, tireless, and enthusiastic advocate for improving the welfare of animals in human care. His EXCELLENCE BEYOND COMPLIANCE program is a unique resource, full of advice and useful tools gleaned from decades of experience, to help those of us dedicated to caring for animals do our very best each day. As he frequently says: 'It's all about the animals.'"

Wendy Bulger, Esq.
General Counsel
San Diego Zoo Global

"Gesualdi's primer is a 'must have' for anyone or any facility attempting to navigate the Animal Welfare Act. His team approach to welfare challenges every staff member to recognize that their performance, no matter what the task, should translate to improving the welfare of the animals in their care. My favorite quote: 'EXCELLENCE BEYOND COMPLIANCE is an ongoing process rather than a destination.' His challenge of continuous improvement takes us from just meeting requirements to developing a culture dedicated to welfare, health and safety for animals and their caregivers."

Yvonne Nadler, DVM, MPH
Consultant to the Zoological community on
all hazards contingency planning

"Mr. Gesualdi has, through his intellect, insight and expertise, provided a balanced and unbiased approach to exceeding the animal welfare regulations. I strongly recommend implementing the guidelines contained within to provide the best care possible for the animals in our stewardship, which, in the end, is what society demands and human nature wills."

Wm. Kirk Suedmeyer, DVM, Dipl. ACZM
Director of Animal Health, The Kansas City Zoo
Past President, American Association of Zoo Veterinarians

"Well done! I always say that regulations and standards prevent both the worst and the best outcomes. So I certainly support *Excellence Beyond Compliance*'s admonition to exceed standards, and the insight that the drive to exceed expectations must become personal before it can become institutional."

Jon Coe, FASLA
Founding Principal
Jon Coe Design, Pty. Ltd.

"*Excellence Beyond Compliance* reveals an attorney demonstrating intense and practical interest in the welfare of animals without relying on an emotionally-charged animal legal 'rights' paradigm. Author James Gesualdi shows respect for all people interested in improving conditions for animals, regardless of their philosophical stances. Having worked with and studied the Animal Welfare Act for nearly 25 years as an attorney, Mr. Gesualdi's deeply practical recommendations for animal caretakers merit serious attention. *Excellence Beyond Compliance* admirably promotes a mindset of going well beyond the AWA's minimum requirements, and it enthusiastically calls on those who work with animals to serve as noble champions of their welfare."

Richard L. Cupp Jr.
John W. Wade Professor of Law
Pepperdine University, School of Law

"Government regulations are typically aimed at establishing minimum standards, and appropriately so. But when it comes to ensuring the quality of life for the animals that we care for, many want to go beyond 'minimum' and strive to achieve 'best.' Thus, the value of *Excellence Beyond Compliance* is to put in place internal mechanisms that utilize the minimum standards and regulatory process under the Animal Welfare Act to achieve excellence in animal care. Ultimately, through the efforts of individuals and institutions striving to achieve excellence, the standard of care improves for all animals."

W. Ron DeHaven, DVM, MBA
Executive Vice President and CEO
American Veterinary Medical Association
(Former Administrator, USDA APHIS)

EXCELLENCE
BEYOND
COMPLIANCE

ENHANCING ANIMAL WELFARE THROUGH THE
CONSTRUCTIVE USE OF THE ANIMAL WELFARE ACT

JAMES F. GESUALDI

MAURICE BASSETT

EXCELLENCE BEYOND COMPLIANCE: Enhancing Animal Welfare Through the Constructive Use of the Animal Welfare Act.

Copyright © 2014 by James F. Gesualdi

James F. Gesualdi is the owner of the trademark EXCELLENCE BEYOND COMPLIANCE.

Excellence Beyond Compliance website:
www.excellencebeyondcompliance.com

Maurice Bassett
P.O. Box 839
Anna Maria, FL 34216-0839

MauriceBassett@gmail.com
www.MauriceBassett.com

For information about bulk order discounts for organizations, please contact the publisher at MauriceBassett@gmail.com

Editing and interior design by Chris Nelson
Cover art by Maria Berg
Cover design by Brian Halley, BookCreatives.com

ISBN-13: 978-1-60025-087-3

Library of Congress Control Number: 2014908219

First Edition

Respect for all life is the foundation.
Kaianrekowa (Great Law of Peace)

Disclaimer

EXCELLENCE BEYOND COMPLIANCE is not, nor is it meant to be, legal advice, and it is certainly not a substitute for current law and agency guidance, or for zoological organizations and zoological professionals being knowledgeable about the Animal Welfare Act (AWA) and the animals in their care. Neither should it replace good legal counsel when such is needed. The opinions expressed herein are solely those of the author.

Author's Note

*I shall pass through this world but once. Any good,
therefore, that I can do or any kindness that I can show
to any fellow creature, let me do it now.*

Stephen Grellet

I love and respect animals.[1] I am privileged to work with people,
zoological organizations and other groups that love animals and
ceaselessly work to care for and protect them both in zoological
settings and in the wild.

*EXCELLENCE BEYOND COMPLIANCE: Enhancing
Animal Welfare Through the Constructive Use of the Animal
Welfare Act* is a manifestation of that love and a personal
commitment to making a difference for animals and people.
EXCELLENCE BEYOND COMPLIANCE represents lessons
learned from nearly a quarter century spent studying and working
with the Animal Welfare Act. If the simple, straightforward ideas
and tools which constitute EXCELLENCE BEYOND
COMPLIANCE help just one more person, zoological
organization, accrediting or professional association or other
stakeholder to meaningfully enhance animal welfare, the effort has
been worthwhile.

I would like to acknowledge here every person I have
worked with, each organization I have served, all the government
officials and others with differing perspectives whom I have

---

[1] The terms "animal" and "animals" as used in this book refer to nonhuman
animals. Nonetheless, it is acknowledged that humans are also animals.

encountered, and every animal we have endeavored to help. All have taught me valuable lessons that inform EXCELLENCE BEYOND COMPLIANCE's constructive approach.

Thanks to Patricia A. Milito for so capably putting this all together in an easily accessible and readily helpful presentation. Catherine Keenan and Thomas Killeen have provided wise counsel. Much appreciation to Chris Nelson for his skillful and extraordinarily thoughtful editing, and to Maurice Bassett for his fearless publishing, which has made this available to the world.

Thanks and love to Valerie, Mariel, Maeve and Memphis for their unending love and support for such efforts, and to my parents and grandparents for getting this journey started.

The dolphin Little Bit provided the inspiration for this work a quarter of a century ago when she opened my heart and transformed my life.

Table of Contents

List of Abbreviations

AC	U.S. Department of Agriculture Animal and Plant Health Inspection Service Animal Care
AIP	Aquarium Improvement Plan
APHIS	U.S. Department of Agriculture Animal and Plant Health Inspection Service
AWA	Animal Welfare Act
AWIC	U.S. Department of Agriculture National Agricultural Library Animal Welfare Information Center
AWIG	*Animal Welfare Inspection Guide*
CFR	Code of Federal Regulations
EBC	EXCELLENCE BEYOND COMPLIANCE
FOIA	Freedom of Information Act
IACUC	Institutional Animal Care and Use Committee
IES	U.S. Department of Agriculture Animal and Plant Health Inspection Service Investigative and Enforcement Services
OGC	U.S. Department of Agriculture Office of General Counsel
OIG	U.S. Department of Agriculture Office of Inspector General
PIP	Park Improvement Plan
SSP	Species Survival Plan®
TAG	Taxon Advisory Group
USC	United States Code
USDA	U.S. Department of Agriculture
ZIP	Zoo Improvement Plan

Preface

Life is full of beginnings. They are presented every day and every hour to every person. Most beginnings are small and appear trivial and insignificant, but in reality they are the most important things in life.

James Allen

People are passionate about animals. This fact is reflected in the many spirited discussions about animal issues taking place today, especially those relating to animals in zoos, aquariums, and marine and wildlife parks (all of which are referred to as "zoological organizations" in this book). These discussions also extend to the subject of how the care and treatment of animals in such organizations should be addressed under the United States Animal Welfare Act (AWA). The discourse involves great ethical and practical concerns, as well as a multitude of stakeholders, many of whom hold strong positions.

Deeper examination shows that within each of the varied perspectives of the regulatory agency, zoological organizations, the public, critics, other animal-related organizations and stakeholders there is an underlying genuine and shared interest in helping animals. Every one of us wants to make a difference. People who care for and about animals are especially motivated to have a positive impact on their lives.

What is EXCELLENCE BEYOND COMPLIANCE?

EXCELLENCE BEYOND COMPLIANCE is a constructive approach to tap our passion and compassion for animals in order to enhance their well-being every day. It is a model, non-regulatory program for zoological organizations seeking to demonstrate an extraordinary commitment to enhancing animal welfare above and beyond the AWA's requirements.

EXCELLENCE BEYOND COMPLIANCE presents a philosophy and plan of action to help achieve this goal for zoological organizations and others responsible for the well-being and safety of animals. The principles and best practices contained in these pages are informed by the AWA and are designed to inspire caregivers and zoological organizations to promote a policy of EXCELLENCE BEYOND COMPLIANCE in their care of animals.

The essential elements of the EXCELLENCE BEYOND COMPLIANCE program include:

- Proactive use of the AWA to enhance animal welfare and promote organizational excellence.
- A philosophy of continuous improvement.
- A top-down/bottom-up commitment.
- A team approach and shared responsibility.
- Use of best practices, procedures, and tools.

EXCELLENCE BEYOND COMPLIANCE strives to consistently focus individual and organizational processes on animal welfare enhancements. It will also serve to make zoological organizations more effective in handling day-to-day regulatory requirements and more adept at preparing for, responding to, and benefiting from the inspection process.[2]

In essence, the practice of EXCELLENCE BEYOND COMPLIANCE involves a paradigm shift. On the one hand it incorporates the AWA's minimum standards and the overlay of

---

[2] Although EXCELLENCE BEYOND COMPLIANCE is designed specifically for use by accredited zoological organizations and other licensed exhibitors operating under the AWA, the principles and approach have much broader application. These tools are likely to be similarly effective when utilized by other regulated entities committed to enhancing animal welfare and promoting organizational excellence. They could also be adapted to other regulatory systems outside the United States, especially those that approximate the AWA.

self-regulation via accreditation. At the same time it encourages individuals and organizations to go beyond these requirements, to adopt a mindset of continuous improvement and heightened awareness regarding the welfare of the animals in their care. It inspires them to act appropriately and effectively as champions of those animals.

Even outstanding zoological organizations and zoological professionals can benefit from adopting EXCELLENCE BEYOND COMPLIANCE as a tool to encourage continued enhancements in animal welfare.

How to Use This Book

This book can be read constructively by anyone engaged with zoological or other regulated communities involving animals, including leadership, staff, volunteers, consultants, supporters, guests/visitors, regulators—even critics. But it is first and foremost intended to serve as a guide for zoological organization board and executive leadership, staff and volunteers. It should be read as supplementing and enhancing, but by no means replacing, federal regulations, agency guidance, and other substantive informational resources. (These latter could include, for example, the standards and guidelines of accrediting associations and Taxon Advisory Group [TAG] recommendations.)

Organizations and professionals applying the principles and best practices detailed in EXCELLENCE BEYOND COMPLIANCE will seamlessly integrate regulations, guidance and additional helpful practices into their daily activities. They will be better prepared to engage with inspections, investigations, serious incidents, and the myriad other challenges and opportunities their work brings them into contact with every day. Most importantly, they will be empowered to take on a greater role not only in ensuring AWA compliance, but in going beyond it to enhance the well-being of the animals in their care.

The EXCELLENCE BEYOND COMPLIANCE approach is designed to be constructive, positive, voluntary, empowering, and even inspirational. It can be adopted gradually or wholesale, depending on need and available resources; a zoological organization can aspire to adopt every aspect of the EXCELLENCE BEYOND COMPLIANCE approach, but it can *start* wherever it makes the most sense.

Never stop until your good becomes better,
and your better becomes the best.

Frank Zappa

You never change things by fighting the existing reality. To change something, build a new model that makes the existing model obsolete.

R. Buckminster Fuller

The best way to predict the future is to create it.

Peter Drucker

I: THE ANIMAL WELFARE ACT AND EXCELLENCE BEYOND COMPLIANCE

If you are going to achieve excellence in big things, you develop the habit in little matters. Excellence is not an exception, it is a prevailing attitude.

Charles R. Swindoll

A Brief Overview of the AWA

The implementation, administration and enforcement of the AWA[3] and its regulations[4] matter. The AWA provides "minimum requirements"[5] for the humane handling, care, treatment and transportation of regulated animal species involved in certain activities, including public exhibition at licensed entities like zoological organizations. The AWA was enacted, and has periodically been amended, by the United States Congress. It is implemented, administered and enforced by the United States Department of Agriculture (USDA) Animal and Plant Health Inspection Service (APHIS) Animal Care (AC). APHIS' policy is to promote "continuous compliance" with the AWA through its use of unannounced inspections, the ongoing education of regulated entities and, as needed, its enforcement authority.

The administrative portion of the AWA regulations contains requirements relating to licensing, inspections, and recordkeeping. The substantive regulations include generally applicable standards for veterinary care and animal handling, and

---

[3] 7 U.S.C. § 2131, et seq.
[4] 9 C.F.R. § 1.1, et seq.
[5] 7 U.S.C. § 2143(a)(2)(1).

specific standards for each of several classes of covered species including: dogs and cats; guinea pigs and hamsters; rabbits; nonhuman primates; marine mammals; and other warm-blooded animals, which of course includes many zoo animals.

Within each category of species and the overall catch-all ("other warm-blooded animals") the regulations refer to indoor and outdoor facilities, space, feeding, sanitation, staffing, a few species-specific elements (e.g., "environmental enhancement to promote psychological well-being" of nonhuman primates[6]), and transport.

These requirements include a mix of engineering and performance-based standards. Engineering standards quantify or specify a requirement—for example, the minimum dimensional measurements for an enclosure. These are more typically "minimum" due to their specificity. Other regulations contain performance standards as requirements; for example, an animal must be handled safely so as to avoid a certain condition. The generalized, outcome-oriented nature of the performance standards makes them more elastic and subject to discretion and interpretation. The broader performance-based standards also create room for creativity and flexibility, which can foster animal welfare-enhancing innovation.

Animal Care works with APHIS Investigative and Enforcement Services (IES) and the USDA Office of General Counsel (OGC) as necessary to enforce the AWA. In the event of serious and/or repeated noncompliances, Animal Care refers a case to IES for investigation and resolution.[7] Animal Care has also created both online and hard copy complaint forms for the public to submit concerns about animals that are covered under the AWA.[8]

---

[6] 9 C.F.R. § 3.81.

[7] See Chapter VII: *Investigations and Enforcement*, and *Appendix F: Enforcement Information*. Note that noncompliances can be resolved via no further action, letter of warning, proposed stipulation of settlement, formal prosecution, consent decree, or full administrative adjudication culminating in sanctions (including fines and license suspension or revocation).

[8] For the hard copy form, see the USDA, APHIS, Animal Care, *Animal Welfare Inspection Guide* (2013) (hereinafter "*Animal Welfare Inspection Guide*"), p A-43, available at: http://www.aphis.usda.gov/animal_welfare/downloads/Animal

Compliance with the AWA regulations is manifested by an inspection report which, in the event of a successful inspection, notes: "No noncompliant items identified during this inspection."[9] Continuous compliance is evidenced by multiple consecutive, fully compliant inspection reports. Such documentation of "continuous compliance" is laudable as it demonstrates that on those particular dates the "animal care inspector" or "veterinary medical officer" (hereinafter "inspector") determined the facility to be fully compliant. As the AWA provides "minimum standards," full and continuous compliance should be a facility's starting point.

EXCELLENCE BEYOND COMPLIANCE

The above overview is intended as a cursory primer or refresher on the process and the substance of the AWA. As noted, the AWA is a "minimum standards" statute and the AWA regulations are often just that: "minimum." The AWA's minimum standards are important, as are the standards and guidelines of accrediting associations, but EXCELLENCE BEYOND COMPLIANCE goes much further in striving to enhance the well-being of animals. It also provides a means whereby organizations can take straightforward, practical steps to maintain compliance with AWA regulations and prepare for inspections and accreditation on an ongoing basis.

%20Care%20Inspection%20Guide.pdf. For the online form, see *USDA, APHIS, Animal Care Animal Welfare Complaint*, available at: http://www.aphis.usda.gov/wps/portal/aphis/ourfocus/animalwelfare/complaint-form

[9] See *Appendix B: Inspection Report Notice*, for a concise explanation of inspection reports, available at:
http://www.aphis.usda.gov/animal_welfare/downloads/IR_Explanation.pdf
Note, "[a] 'Direct' noncompliance is a noncompliance that is currently adversely affecting the health and well-being of the animal, or has the high potential to adversely affect the health and well-being of the animal in the near or immediate future." *Animal Welfare Inspection Guide, at 2-5.*

Elevating AWA Compliance and Animal Welfare

Zoological organizations, licensed as exhibitors under the AWA, have long proclaimed their missions to include animal welfare, animal or wildlife conservation, research in furtherance of animal welfare and wildlife conservation, associated conservation education and, in some cases, wildlife rescue. Consistent with these commitments, compliance with the AWA is vitally important. Those organizations which seek to harmonize and reinforce their mission and public messaging should broaden their efforts to incorporate EXCELLENCE BEYOND COMPLIANCE. This may provide for a participating organization to make a much stronger presentation during regulatory reviews of a facility but, more importantly, it is essential for enhancing animal welfare.

Simply put, better organizations commit daily to enhanced animal welfare, and by so doing live their mission in a most compelling manner. Most importantly, the animals which zoological organizations exist to serve benefit. As Terry L. Maple and Bonnie M. Perdue write in *Zoo Animal Welfare*:

> If we elevate its visibility and its priority, the welfare of zoo animals is bound to improve. The institutional mission statement must articulate and affirm core values that support animal care and welfare.[10]

Getting Started

Animal welfare, as defined by the Association of Zoos and Aquariums Animal Welfare Committee, is paramount.

---

[10] Terry L. Maple & Bonnie M. Perdue, *Zoo Animal Welfare* (Heidelberg: Springer, 2013). Maple and Perdue provide an indispensable resource for zoological organizations committed to enhancing animal welfare. The book contains a comprehensive review of animal welfare and the associated scientific literature, as well as relevant considerations and factors contributing to animal welfare; e.g., welfare metrics, psychology, environmental enrichment, behavior and design. For additional resources, see also Center for Zoo Animal Welfare, available at: http://czaw.org/ and Chicago Zoological Society, Centers of Excellence, Center for Animal Welfare, available at: https://czs.org/czs/csaw

Animal Welfare refers to an animal's collective physical, mental, and emotional states over a period of time, and is measured on a continuum from good to poor.

Explanation: An animal typically experiences good welfare when healthy, comfortable, well-nourished, safe, able to develop and express species-typical relationships, behaviors, and cognitive abilities, and not suffering from unpleasant states such as pain, fear, or distress. Because physical, mental, and emotional states may be dependent on one another and can vary from day to day, it is important to consider these states in combination with one another over time to provide an assessment of an animal's overall welfare status.[11]

EXCELLENCE BEYOND COMPLIANCE begins with a commitment to fostering and maintaining AWA compliance and continuously improving efforts towards enhancing animal welfare. That commitment must be clear and unequivocal and extend from the bottom up and the top down. It must be an explicit, universal, organizational objective. Leadership and staff must understand this on day one and remain mindful daily.

Skillfully and caringly operating an outstanding zoological organization presents numerous challenges. When embraced as opportunities to move towards excellence, these challenges help to develop and improve an organization. Engaging and transforming such challenges becomes second nature when an organization and its staff strive every day to provide the best possible animal welfare and continually seek new ways to further improve the organization. Acting in this fashion is the best way to demonstrate an extraordinary commitment to the animals in their care and— through conservation efforts and education messaging—to those in the wild.

---

[11] See Association of Zoos and Aquariums, Animal Welfare Committee, available at: http://www.aza.org/membership/detail.aspx?id=378. Defining and discussing "animal welfare" is in itself an important and worthy endeavor on the road to enhancing animal welfare.

Words, Actions, Culture

EXCELLENCE BEYOND COMPLIANCE begins with an awareness of its central concepts that is then put into words and carried out daily by every member of the zoological organization's staff, volunteer corps and leadership until those words and actions establish (or enhance) a constructive culture which supports and reinforces the primacy of animal welfare. Such an organizational culture fosters creativity, innovation and shared responsibility for all aspects of animal welfare. Everything that happens at a zoological organization ultimately connects to and reflects upon the standard of animal welfare.

EXCELLENCE BEYOND COMPLIANCE is an ongoing process rather than a destination. As such, even the best of organizations may occasionally fall short of the minimum standards under the AWA. These shortcomings may have consequences for animals, people and organizations. In such situations the primary concern should be to remedy the immediate situation in order to protect those impacted by it. Immediately afterwards an honest and constructive examination of what happened should take place, and this review should encompass why and how the situation came about, how it can be prevented from happening again, and what other steps can be undertaken to enhance conditions for any affected animals—and possibly for other animals as well. These steps might include further improvement of facilities, refinement of protocols, modifications in staffing and training, and may even include measures not necessarily directly related to causal elements.

In other words, zoological organizations committed to EXCELLENCE BEYOND COMPLIANCE remain accountable for compliance, but the review of noncompliances, if any, as well as existing conditions generally, should be used constructively towards continuously enhancing animal welfare.

Every Day Matters

Any and every day could conceivably be the day before or of an inspection. And for the resident animals housed in a zoological organization there are no "off" days—even the day after a "clean" inspection where no noncompliances were identified. Every day the animals in zoological care warrant the best that a zoological organization has to offer. EXCELLENCE BEYOND COMPLIANCE helps provide it to them.

When you grow up in an environment where . . . commitment and dedication is not just talked about but lived so fully, so honestly, there is no way that it does not take root in your being.

Yolanda King

Your only limitation is how much action you are willing to take.

Carrie Wilkerson

II: ORGANIZATIONAL FRAMEWORK

Let each of us work to build organizations where everyone can make a contribution – where everybody counts – organizations which will continue to change the world.

Elizabeth Dole

Excellence is not a spectator sport. Everyone's involved.

Jack Welch

1.   *Every individual can make a difference*

Everyone is a member of the "AWA Compliance Team" and the EXCELLENCE BEYOND COMPLIANCE effort. AWA compliance, animal welfare, and EXCELLENCE BEYOND COMPLIANCE are everyone's responsibility, every day. Everyone, every day. A lapse in nearly any area or department can potentially impact AWA compliance and animal welfare. Everyone should be aware of this and of the importance of "little things" they can do every day. For example, anyone working at a zoological organization can pick up stray litter or debris which could wind up in an animal enclosure (or notify someone who can). Staff can flag inappropriate guest behavior or alert others as to observations about animals or facilities needing attention. In addition to staff training, providing staff (as well as volunteers) with laminated checklists or cards to carry can improve both the quality and quantity of observations. Such checklists could indicate the types of appearances, behaviors or conditions warranting a closer look by appropriate staff.

2.   *Everyone shares responsibility for animal welfare*

Collaboration is a key element in ensuring animal welfare. Even across animal-related departments and different units, every person must understand that individually and together they are all part of the zoological organization team, and that they all share responsibility for AWA compliance, animal welfare, and EXCELLENCE BEYOND COMPLIANCE. For example, it is not uncommon to read an inspection report where a noncompliance is as much related to a construction or maintenance issue as it is to an animal caregiving one. Zoological organization leadership should therefore constantly encourage, recognize and reward individuals and groups of staff who work well with others, including different units, to reinforce the importance of the EXCELLENCE BEYOND COMPLIANCE effort.

Leadership

3.   *Compliance Officer*

Every zoological organization should have a designated "Compliance Officer" to ensure that shared responsibility for AWA compliance, animal welfare, and EXCELLENCE BEYOND COMPLIANCE does not evolve into a situation where no one is ultimately responsible. It is probably best if this individual is the organization's point of contact for APHIS inspections. In addition, this Compliance Officer must be extremely knowledgeable about the AWA regulations and animal welfare. Significantly, the Compliance Officer must have an appropriate degree of organizational authority that allows them to carry out their responsibilities and ensure AWA compliance and EXCELLENCE BEYOND COMPLIANCE. Part of this individual's responsibility will include organizing training, maintaining compliance between inspections and communicating as appropriate to follow up internally and with the agency.

4.   *Animal Welfare Officer*

Every zoological organization should have a designated, executive level "Animal Welfare Officer." The Animal Welfare Officer is responsible for monitoring, promoting and enhancing animal welfare and related management and planning in coordination with the Compliance Officer and the Animal Welfare Leadership Group (see below). The Compliance Officer and the Animal Welfare Officer can be the same person, and that person may hold another title, but these are two distinct but overlapping and mutually reinforcing positions. The Animal Welfare Officer must be knowledgeable about animal welfare and skilled in interpersonal relations such that they are both respected and approachable by other staff. While the Compliance Officer focuses on the AWA, its regulations and related processes (which have animal welfare components), the Animal Welfare Officer focuses entirely on animals and their welfare. To maximize and validate effectiveness, the Animal Welfare Officer should also help coordinate the organization's animal welfare-centered research efforts, whether conducted by in-house staff or in cooperation with outside researchers.

5.   *Animal Welfare Leadership Group*

Even the most knowledgeable and talented Compliance Officer and Animal Welfare Officer are going to have limited expertise or understanding of certain zoological areas, activities or operations. Therefore, every zoological organization should have a designated "Animal Welfare Leadership Group". (Some zoological organizations may already have an Animal Welfare Committee that could be modified or expanded to serve as the Animal Welfare Leadership Group.) The functioning of the Animal Welfare Leadership Group is somewhat similar to the Institutional Animal Care and Use Committee (IACUC) required for registered research facilities, but it is voluntary, less formal and has a broader role with respect to AWA compliance and enhancing animal welfare generally.[12] For zoological organizations with an IACUC, the

---

[12] For more information on IACUCs see 9 C.F.R. § 2.31 and *Animal Welfare Inspection Guide* at 7-1 to 7-60.

Animal Welfare Leadership Group can be an adjunct or supplement to the IACUC's role with regard to regulated research activities.

The Animal Welfare Leadership Group is intended to include a cross section of high level staff in order to facilitate collaborative action on animal welfare and AWA matters. It oversees the EXCELLENCE BEYOND COMPLIANCE program and should have broad authority to review and shape all animal-related activities. An Animal Welfare Leadership Group should, to the extent possible given the nature and size of the organization, include:

- Caregivers, including behavioral/husbandry/training staff.
- An attending veterinarian.
- Buildings and grounds staff.
- Maintenance staff.
- Researchers.
- Other staff or even volunteers, as appropriate.

Other staff should be incorporated if helpful at a given facility, perhaps including, but not limited to, the Safety Officer, who is typically responsible for risk management and the safety program. Such broad representation underscores the depth of this effort and ensures that relevant management and staff are fully invested in making the organization function at a level beyond simple compliance. Where a zoological organization is open to other perspectives, consideration should be given to including representatives from outside the organization, possibly including consultants, recognized experts and independent members.

One of the simplest and most effective activities for the Animal Welfare Leadership Group is having regularly scheduled meetings and rounds to review the animals and facilities. Having a set schedule, established well in advance, makes it easier for all staff to prepare and participate. It also empowers front line staff to be ready for rounds. In short, this is a foundational building block that can offer broad benefits to the organization and the animals in its care.

6.   *Internal reporting to the Chief Executive*

The Compliance Officer, Animal Welfare Officer and Animal Welfare Leadership Group should report directly to the zoological organization's Chief Executive. This ensures that AWA compliance, animal welfare, and EXCELLENCE BEYOND COMPLIANCE are appropriately formalized and supported at the highest levels of the organization.

Responsibilities

7.   *Adoption of the EXCELLENCE BEYOND COMPLIANCE program*

Ideally, the EXCELLENCE BEYOND COMPLIANCE program should be formally adopted by the zoological organization's board or leadership. This demonstrates extraordinary organizational commitment to the approach and tools essential for successful implementation. It is also possible for the program to be adopted into practice one caregiver or department at a time, should this ultimately prove more feasible given a particular organization's existing culture and structure. The point is getting moving in the right direction.

8.   *Implementation of the EXCELLENCE BEYOND COMPLIANCE program*

The Compliance Officer, Animal Welfare Officer, and Animal Welfare Leadership Group should develop and implement the EXCELLENCE BEYOND COMPLIANCE program. This underscores the commitment of zoological-wide leadership and staff to the successful implementation of EXCELLENCE BEYOND COMPLIANCE.

9.   *Review proposed changes to existing operating principles and activities*

The Compliance Officer, Animal Welfare Officer, and Animal Welfare Leadership Group should review all significant proposed changes in animal welfare practices, animal-related activities, facilities and operations. Some improvements and organizational interventions may require longer-term horizons. For example, with respect to the construction of new facilities and the substantial renovation of existing ones, the Animal Welfare Leadership Group's role should extend from thoughtful, animal-friendly design through to post-completion of projects. This ensures such facilities best serve animal welfare and the staff responsible for caring for the animals. It also guarantees an AWA-centric review at the earliest practical moment and throughout the process (to the extent possible). This measure, like most of the operating principles of EXCELLENCE BEYOND COMPLIANCE, is intended to avoid preventable errors, further enhance animal welfare, and accelerate organizational advancement.

10.   Animal Welfare Plan

Every zoological organization should consider the development and adoption of an Animal Welfare Plan upon initiating an EXCELLENCE BEYOND COMPLIANCE program. The Animal Welfare Plan would establish goals, benchmarks, resources and tools for animal welfare-related activities. Such a plan can start modestly, perhaps focusing on certain animals or species. It should include baseline data for existing conditions and provide a means for assessing progress and validating results. (Animal welfare-related personnel, as well as research staff or outside researchers are thus vitally important to the development, implementation and evaluation of the Animal Welfare Plan.) Whatever the specific results are, they will yield insights into whether certain measures are effective; if they are not, alternatives can be developed in search of enhancements.

11.   Extend the EXCELLENCE BEYOND COMPLIANCE program to include all resident-animal species

While the AWA only covers mammals (and birds, though there are not yet any bird-specific regulations) involved in regulated activities like exhibition, zoological organizations should consider extending AWA-like protections and the animal welfare program to all resident animal species. This is especially meaningful in underscoring the depth of commitment to enhancing animal welfare and may further harmonize with conservation activities and messaging on behalf of species not regulated under the AWA.

12. *Research to enhance animal welfare*

Every zoological organization should undertake, participate in and support meaningful, science-based research to further advance animal welfare. Engaging in such research is essential for attaining baseline states of welfare, validating the effectiveness of welfare-related improvements, and discovering, refining and confirming further enhancements to such measures. Voluntarily undertaking, participating in and supporting such research guarantees accelerated advances in enhancing animal welfare.[13] Even small, simple efforts can add up to a meaningful, cumulative impact each year, and improvements are further compounded over time.

Training

13. *General training*

All manner of staff training must consist of initial, ongoing and periodic training components. It is essential that comprehensive training be provided upon hire or organizational commitment to EXCELLENCE BEYOND COMPLIANCE. Concurrent with training, all zoological organization staff should be instructed and reminded about the overriding importance of animal welfare, the AWA and EXCELLENCE BEYOND COMPLIANCE.

---

[13] One such example of collaborative research is a recent multi-institution elephant welfare study. This three-year project examined hundreds of elephants in North American zoos, amassing significant amounts of data that will contribute directly to enhancing elephant welfare. Public Communications (PCI), "Enhancing zoo elephant welfare," ScienceDaily (September 10, 2013), available at: http://www.sciencedaily.com/releases/2013/09/130910205244.htm

14.   Ongoing training

Initial training is not enough. Brief, informal annual training and written reminder statements of organizational policy and commitment make explicit the importance of these principles and keep them current. Training in animal welfare, the AWA and EXCELLENCE BEYOND COMPLIANCE must be ongoing so as to imprint and reinforce knowledge and organizational commitment and to incorporate new information and advanced understanding. There should also be periodic refresher or updated training.

15.   Supplemental training for staff directly involved with animal care and welfare

Zoological organization animal welfare, behavioral/ husbandry/training, veterinary, buildings and grounds, maintenance, and other staff whose work more directly impacts animal welfare should receive additional in-depth training on the AWA and inspections. This training should relate their daily responsibilities to general and specific regulatory requirements as well as to how performance may be assessed during an inspection. The primary focus should remain on animal welfare, with a secondary emphasis on the regulatory process as a means for validating good work and fostering further ongoing improvement. This training would also help sensitize staff to the measures and records important to note or present during inspections. Internal reviews or rounds may present opportunities to include hands-on components in the training program.

It is also important to include staff training and development in animal behavior. The availability of staff, specialists or consultants knowledgeable about the behaviors of resident species (both housed at zoological organizations and in the wild) can provide valuable perspectives to enhance animal welfare.

16.   Outside professional development activities

All staff, including caregiving (e.g., behavioral/ husbandry/training and veterinary), buildings and grounds, maintenance, and others, should be encouraged, recognized and rewarded for undertaking relevant professional development activities on their own (and/or with zoological organization support). Zoological organizations should encourage, facilitate, fund, and permit as much meaningful professional development as staff members genuinely seek to undertake to further their knowledge and skills. Specific formulas, policies, incentives and recognition programs should be considered to promote initiative in professional development. Highest priority should be given to activities that directly advance animal welfare and further develop associated staff capabilities and expertise. Other activities serving the needs and interests of animals, such as animal rescue, wildlife conservation, conservation education and research, are also valuable, particularly when harmoniously integrated into animal welfare efforts at the zoological organization.

Empowering Staff

17.   *Caregiving staff*

Most zoological organization staff and (and even volunteers) are dedicated and passionate about their work. They are often the best un- or under-tapped resources for simple yet effective ideas for enriching animal lives, improving facilities or other practices. Staff (and volunteers) should be encouraged, recognized and rewarded for ideas and teamwork evidencing awareness of and shared responsibility for animal welfare. In essence, all staff is caregiving staff.

18.   *Internal organizational challenges, concerns and staff input*

Internal organizational challenges should be identified and addressed as soon as possible, and all staff should be encouraged to express reasonable—however modest—concerns and constructive suggestions. Seemingly isolated instances of animal illness or death, or of housekeeping or maintenance issues, may appear at any time and in the absence of inspections or internal organizational reviews. If there is a possibility that there could be more to a given situation than initially meets the eye, the zoological organization should undertake a review. The zoological organization might even formalize a means for submitting such concerns (including externally-generated ones) and having them reviewed and acted upon, perhaps by the Animal Welfare Leadership Group. Constructively utilizing and valuing legitimate expressions of concern may help to avoid bigger challenges and accelerate preventive and positive action.

> *The secret of joy in work is contained in one word – excellence. To know how to do something well is to enjoy it.*
>
> **Pearl S. Buck**

> *Commitment shows up in action. I know what people are committed to, it's what they're doing.*
>
> **Steve Chandler**

III: BEFORE AN INSPECTION

Let us not be content to wait and see what will happen, but give us the determination to make the right things happen.

Horace Mann

1.   *Developing an EXCELLENCE BEYOND COMPLIANCE protocol*

The Compliance Officer, Animal Welfare Officer, and the Animal Welfare Leadership Group should collaboratively develop an EXCELLENCE BEYOND COMPLIANCE protocol for handling regulatory inspections. This will maximize the effectiveness of a zoological organization's commitment to AWA compliance, animal welfare, and EXCELLENCE BEYOND COMPLIANCE. The protocol should provide for the implementation of the tools set forth in EXCELLENCE BEYOND COMPLIANCE, as well as for other measures unique to the zoological organization, including direction as to how these ideas will be put into practice in preparing for and handling inspections.

2.   *Different types of inspections*

The information in this section is largely directed towards the regularly occurring routine inspection process. As noted in the *Animal Welfare Inspection Guide*, there are several kinds of inspections.[14] Unannounced routine inspections also include reinspections, those related to complaints, and those which are focused on specific items or on a particular part of a facility. Other types of inspections include attempted inspections (where a facility

---

[14] See *Animal Welfare Inspection Guide* at 3-18.

representative is not present or refuses entry), pre-license inspections and different types of specialized facility inspections, including those for animal rides, complaints, drive-through zoos, lion and tiger enclosures, petting zoos, photo shoots and travelling exhibitors.[15]

The one kind of inspection referenced in the *Animal Welfare Inspection Guide* under both routine and specific types of inspections is the complaint inspection. All zoological organizations should be familiar with the agency complaint forms and process.[16]

In preparing for inspections, zoological organizations should educate themselves on the different types of inspections and how the agency conducts them. Understanding the different factors which may frame a particular inspection will enable a zoological organization to appropriately prepare for and undergo inspections.

Note that such awareness, and the recommendations below, can also be helpful for handling investigations (discussed in Chapter VII) as well as inspections.

Internal Review and Mock Inspections

3.   *Internal review of animals and facilities*

The Animal Welfare Leadership Group should conduct monthly or at least quarterly rounds of the zoological organization's resident animals and facilities. Any items warranting attention or improvement, whether seemingly compliant or not, should be identified and addressed. More complex or substantial items should be evaluated and resolved within designated time frames. This group or the Compliance Officer must then confirm and perhaps document the successful completion of any follow up measures.

The frequency of these rounds can vary according to the nature and size of an organization's facilities, but they should occur at least quarterly (which is also helpful in ensuring reviews

---

[15] See *Animal Welfare Inspection Guide* at Chapter 4.

[16] See, e.g., *Animal Welfare Inspection Guide* at 4-15 to 4-17 (discussing complaint process).

during different times of the year). Larger organizations may schedule rounds for one portion of the facility at a time to make this process more manageable. Organizations engaged in more dramatic transformation should, if at all possible, conduct monthly rounds until substantial progress is evident.

Note: At some organizations, records relating to these efforts may be subject to disclosure under local, state or federal freedom of information laws, and also might be requested by APHIS during an inspection or investigation. This possibility may be sufficient to discourage such conscientious and ongoing organizational self-examination. It may prompt some to do such rounds but to refrain from keeping written records. In any event, even if the use of such records out of context might seem to invite criticism, the generation of those records must be understood as a necessary component in organizational advancement, particularly with respect to animal welfare. Consequently, such internal self-examination and reporting should be encouraged rather than effectively penalized by casual disclosure of corrective measures or improvements undertaken without an explicit regulatory directive to do so. If an organization has concerns in this regard, it should consider consulting counsel.

4. Mock inspections

The Animal Welfare Leadership Group or simply the Compliance Officer and the Animal Welfare Officer should conduct at least one unannounced mock inspection annually (in addition to the regular rounds). This is an additional means of maintaining vigilance as to continuous compliance and animal welfare. This is especially important in years between accreditation inspections for accredited zoological organizations. Another highly effective form of mock inspection involves having the animal care and other staff self-inspect their areas of responsibility, or even other areas, to give them an enhanced, hands-on perspective on the impact of their work on AWA compliance and animal welfare. Staff inspection of animals and facilities they do not normally work with can foster greater appreciation of the work of other staff, as well as cross-fertilization of ideas and a stronger team spirit.

5.   *Using agency guidance for effective mock inspections and rounds*

Using agency guidance will maximize the consistency, quality and usefulness of unannounced mock inspections and rounds. Make use of the *Animal Welfare Inspection Guide* (2013). One particular area to review is the "Inspection Steps" steps at 2-3, which provide:

> Basic steps to follow in conducting an inspection of a facility include, but are **not** limited to:
>
> - Consider problems that may occur at other times of the year.
> - For big cats, ensure that all primary enclosures can safely contain the cats. Also review the feeding plan to assure adequate nutrition.
> - Inspect the animals, premises, building(s), enclosures, equipment, and transportation vehicles/equipment for all pertinent requirements of the regulations and standards.
> - Review previous reports with special attention to Veterinary Care and Direct Noncompliant Items (NCIs).
> - Review the facility's program of veterinary care, husbandry practices, required records and, when appropriate, the "Exercise Plan" for dogs and the "Plan for Environmental Enhancement" for nonhuman primates. When possible, observe the animal handling techniques of facility personnel.[17]

Note: See also below in this chapter, items 14-16.

6.   *Retrospective review of zoological organization inspection reports*

The Compliance Officer and Animal Welfare Officer should review and report on any patterns or recommended measures following a review of ten years' worth of the zoological organization's inspection reports. This retrospective review may yield little if there have been clean or mostly clean inspection

---

[17] See *Animal Welfare Inspection Guide* at 2-3.

reports (which would also indicate a limited number of items to re-examine). Or it might yield a treasure trove of information if there are numbers or patterns of noncompliances. Such review could provide the impetus to address areas needing attention or wholesale reinvention, rather than mere case-by-case fixes. Oftentimes, reviews of more immediate pressing challenges facing a zoological organization indicate that the causes were in play and evident in the inspection history. Enlightened zoological organizations should not need a regulatory or other crisis to prompt retrospective review.

7.   *Retrospective review of inspection reports from other facilities*

The Compliance Officer and Animal Welfare Officer should review and report on any patterns or recommended measures following a review of inspection reports from other facilities using the animal care inspection report database. The database is available online.[18] It can be searched using specific criteria to isolate reviews of, for example, inspections of similar zoological organizations, regulated entities within the same state, those found noncompliant with a particular regulatory section, or inspections from a certain period. Using this database for review provides an external reality check beyond what a zoological organization may discern from interactions with outside colleagues, other zoological organizations, or accrediting and other professional associations. Note also that comprehensive reviews often yield insights into emerging animal welfare issues and regulatory focus. Discovering and understanding emerging issues further enables zoological organizations to undertake proactive measures towards AWA compliance and enhancing animal welfare.

---

[18] See APHIS inspection reports, available at:
http://acissearch.aphis.usda.gov/LPASearch/faces/Warning.jspx;jsessionid=7f00
000130df470de7976c2549aea70fed0799efbf39.e38Obx8Sb3yQby0LbN8Saxm
Ra3mTe0

8.   Review of current and ongoing events

The Compliance Officer and Animal Welfare Officer should review and report on any patterns or recommended measures following a review of current and ongoing events within the zoological community. AWA inspections and zoological organizations are impacted by high-profile situations where the regulations may have been at issue. These events should also prompt immediate internal review and re-examination of similar situations within the zoological organization. [19] This may lead to supplemental training and protocol or facilities upgrades.

9.   Review of forms, policies and protocols

The Compliance Officer and Animal Welfare Officer should periodically have relevant staff assist in the review and updating of zoological organization forms, policies and protocols, especially if these are not already reviewed and updated on an ongoing basis. Experience and zoological organization or community advances should constantly be incorporated into this process to make certain that essential and required policies and protocols exist, are current, and utilize best practices, whether arising from accrediting or other professional associations, a Species Survival Plan® (SSP), Taxon Advisory Groups (TAGs), scientific literature or APHIS guidance or informational resources. Every form, policy and protocol should be reviewed and re-assessed at least once every three years, if not more frequently. The materials reviewed should include everything with AWA compliance and animal welfare consequences. One example of an overlooked type of form is the work-order request submitted by animal caregivers to buildings and grounds or maintenance staff. This form, for example, should be reviewed collaboratively so that

---

[19] One example is "big cat" safety and containment. See, e.g., James F. Gesualdi, "Transforming Tragedy Into Constructive Lessons To Protect People And Animals." New York State Bar Association Committee on Animals and the Law, *Laws & Paws*, 80-94 (March, 2011), available at:
http://www.nysba.org/workarea/DownloadAsset.aspx?id=26307
Note that updated, detailed guidance has since been issued by USDA APHIS. See *Animal Welfare Inspection Guide*, Lion and Tiger Enclosure Heights and Kick-Ins Inspection at 4-26.

all staff are on the same page as to the importance and timing of corrective and preventive work.

10. Confirming proper use of forms, policies and protocols

The Compliance Officer and Animal Welfare Officer should periodically have relevant staff assist in confirming proper use and implementation of zoological organization forms, policies and protocols. Zoological organizations may be held accountable for following (or failing to follow) their own written forms, policies and protocols, especially when something has gone wrong. It is therefore important to monitor internal compliance with an organization's own standards. This should be done on an ongoing basis, and at least semi-annually.

11. Animal Welfare Leadership Group annual report

Annually, the Animal Welfare Leadership Group should report on all animal welfare and compliance-related improvements and modifications implemented by the zoological organization. The greater the advances undertaken, the more impressive the report. This report simply memorializes all the work, primarily voluntarily undertaken, to foster compliance and enhance animal welfare.

12. Outside expertise and assistance

Even outstanding zoological organizations may lack experience or expertise in some areas or might benefit from fresh perspectives. Seeking counsel from experts or other forms of help, whether from within or outside of the zoological community, could accelerate improvement and resolution of animal welfare matters. An organization need not wait for a crisis, an extensive and hyper-critical media story or a voluminous inspection report before seeking such assistance. Being proactive demonstrates that a zoological organization is so committed to the animals in its care that it willingly seeks outside expertise before external critics or challenges force its hand.

Outside assistance can come from recognized experts, especially specialized behavioral/wildlife researchers, consultants, professional peers, accrediting or professional associations and similar groups.[20] Information, experience, and expertise acquired from such external sources can also be incorporated into the forms, policies and protocols discussed above, further demonstrating organizational commitment to continuous improvement.

13.   *Developing an "inspection checklist" for the "entrance briefing"*

The constructive value of regulatory inspections is greatly enhanced when a Compliance Officer has a well-thought-out and organized checklist of items the zoological organization wants to be certain to cover. Therefore, the Compliance Officer, in consultation with the Animal Welfare Officer, should maintain an up-to-date running list of items to discuss with the inspector at the beginning of the next inspection, creating an "inspection checklist" to be used to present an "entrance briefing" to the inspector. Items to be noted on such a checklist and at the beginning of the inspection include:

- Update on corrections to any prior noncompliant items, including making available any supporting materials for "self-certified compliance reporting," as discussed in Chapter VI: *After an Inspection*, items 4, 6 and 7, and Chapter X: *Agency Measures*, items 3-5.
- Overview of any noteworthy improvements or modifications in zoological organization activities, facilities, operations, staff and training since last inspection.
- Questions or requests for guidance from the inspector with respect to any particular situations or potential plans.

---

[20] There are many such quality organizations, including, but not limited to, the Association of Zoos and Aquariums, Alliance of Marine Mammal Parks and Aquariums, American Association of Zoo Horticulture, American Association of Zoo Keepers, American Association of Zoo Veterinarians, American Veterinary Medical Association, Animal Behavior Management Alliance, Elephant Managers Association, and International Marine Animal Trainers' Association.

- Questions for the inspector regarding any changes or updates in agency guidance or practices relevant to the zoological organization.
- Any other special situations (e.g., animals receiving critical care, pregnant or nursing females, new arrivals, deaths, staff changes).
- Any areas or situations of particular interest or concern to the inspector (to be determined through discussion with inspector either prior to or at the time of the "entrance briefing").

Note that any time-sensitive developments should be discussed with the inspector as soon as possible via telephone, rather than waiting for the next inspection.

Agency Expertise and Knowledge

In creating the AWA, Congress bestowed important regulatory responsibilities on the Secretary of Agriculture, who in turn delegated these to APHIS Animal Care. The agency's exercise of its broad discretion is generally accorded deference by the courts and third parties. Consequently, agency guidance is vitally important.

14.   Online resources for agency guidance

Zoological organization staff, including the Compliance Officer, Animal Welfare Officer, and Animal Welfare Leadership Group, should make use of extensive agency,[21] Center for Animal Welfare,[22] and Animal Welfare Information Center ("AWIC")[23] guidance and informational resources available online. These

---

[21] See USDA, APHIS, Animal Care, available at:

http://www.aphis.usda.gov/wps/portal/aphis/ourfocus/animalwelfare

[22] See Center for Animal Welfare, available at: http://www.aphis.usda.gov/ wps/portal/?urile=wcm%3apath%3a%2Faphis_content_library%2Fsa_our_focus %2Fsa_animal_welfare%2Fsa_caw%2Fct_caw_program_info

[23] See Animal Welfare Information Center, available at:

http://awic.nal.usda.gov/

resources include a voluminous inspection guide,[24] policy manual,[25] and other materials (e.g., Tech Notes), all available online and at no cost.[26] These materials should be consulted and incorporated as part of ongoing professional development and staff training. Consistent and productive use of these materials diminishes the likelihood of needing to refer to them for the first time during a crisis or dispute.

15.   Seeking agency guidance

Zoological organizations looking for more information on certain situations, or those developing new facilities and programs, should proactively seek constructive agency guidance when appropriate. Requesting such guidance could begin with a conversation with the zoological organization's inspector or by contacting the regional or headquarters office in order to be directed to the appropriate agency staff. Agency (including Center for Animal Welfare) review early in the development process can identify and help avoid problems before they pose AWA compliance or animal welfare challenges. To the extent that agency resources allow for such review, such practice is highly recommended. This review may allow for guidance not expressly within the regulations but which could potentially alter a project and enhance animal welfare.

16.   Seeking species specialist guidance

When appropriate, it may be helpful for zoological organizations to consult or seek Center for Animal Welfare species

---

[24] See *Animal Welfare Inspection Guide.*

[25] *Animal Care Policy Manual* (March 7, 2014). Note: The link for this version is currently unavailable. Please see the APHIS Stakeholder Registry notice updating Policy 3, available at: http://content.govdelivery.com/accounts/ USDAAPHIS/bulletins/aafd1c. The original Animal Care Resource Guide Policies (March 25, 2011) is available at: http://www.aphis.usda.gov/ animal_welfare/downloads/Animal%20Care%20Policy%20Manual.pdf

[26] See Publications, Forms and Guidance Documents, available at: http:// www.aphis.usda.gov/wps/portal/aphis/ourfocus/animalwelfare/sa_publications/ct_ publications_and_guidance_documents/!ut/p/a0/04_Sj9CPykssy0xPLMnMz0vM AfGjzOK9_D2MDJ0MjDzd3V2dDDz93HwCzL29jAyCzfQLsh0VAbJgL_A!/

specialist guidance when a zoological organization desires additional input on AWA compliance and animal welfare. The Center for Animal Welfare species specialists cover many animals, such as big cats, elephants, marine mammals, and nonhuman primates.[27] This can be especially helpful both in the absence of or in advance of crisis situations. Oftentimes discussing new facilities or plans early in the process can yield helpful suggestions on design or operational features based upon agency reviews or experiences with recurring issues.[28]

[27] See Center for Animal Welfare / Meet the Center, available at:
http://www.aphis.usda.gov/wps/portal/aphis/ourfocus/animalwelfare?1dmy&uril e=wcm%3apath%3a%2Faphis_content_library%2Fsa_our_focus%2Fsa_animal _welfare%2Fsa_caw%2Fct_caw_meet_the_center

[28] See, e.g., considerations relating to pool color and shade features for pinniped facilities with regard to eye health, in Laurie J. Gage, Invited Commentary, "Captive Pinniped Eye Problems, We Can do Better!", 4(2) *J Marine Animals & Their Ecology*, 25-8 (2011), available at:
http://www.oers.ca/journal/volume4/issue2/Gage_Galley.pdf

IV: DURING AN INSPECTION

Success is the sum of small efforts
repeated day in and day out.

Robert Collier

1.   The Golden Rule

Inspectors should be treated professionally and with respect, especially under the most challenging circumstances. This has basis in law, namely the regulations, and in basic human relations.[29] Mutually respectful, ethical and professional conduct eliminates or minimizes extraneous factors not necessarily relevant to the AWA, animal welfare, or the inspection. It also fosters a better likelihood of constructive dialogue whereby emerging concerns might be identified and remedied. Moreover, there is absolutely nothing to be gained by disregarding this "golden rule."

2.   Inspection checklist and entrance briefing

As noted earlier, the Compliance Officer and Animal Welfare Officer should create and review the inspection checklist and engage the inspector in an initial entrance briefing. It is enormously helpful and valuable for the zoological organization to review important information updates and concerns with the

---

[29] As for the AWA regulations, see, e.g., 9 C.F.R. §§ 2.3 "Demonstration of compliance with standards and regulations," 2.4 "Non-interference with APHIS officials," 2.125 "Information as to business; furnishing of same by dealers, exhibitors, operators of auction sales, intermediate handlers, and carriers," and 2.126 "Access and inspection of records and property; submission of itineraries."

inspector at the outset. This helps the zoological organization to make the most of the inspector's time and expertise while they are on site. It also demonstrates to the inspector the organization's awareness of its own operations and its commitment to AWA compliance and animal welfare.

3.   *Organizational representation during inspections*

To the greatest extent possible, the Animal Welfare Leadership Group (or at least a representative subset) should be present or on standby for the entire inspection. This is one of the most effective tools for EXCELLENCE BEYOND COMPLIANCE. It speaks volumes for the zoological organization's commitment to AWA compliance and animal welfare. It makes certain that the relevant staff expertise is present or available throughout the inspection. This in turn allows for informed and immediate response as necessary and facilitates the determination of deliverable correction dates when they are needed. It also gives the zoological organization a more complete view of the inspection. The staff areas represented during the inspection will also develop an enhanced appreciation for AWA issues and inspector concerns. In the alternative, if unable to participate in the inspection, all members of the Animal Welfare Leadership Group should be available for consultation during or immediately after the inspection, perhaps during the exit briefing or at a subsequent internal staff debriefing.

4.   *Share expertise with the inspector*

The Compliance Officer, Animal Welfare Officer, and Animal Welfare Leadership Group should use the inspection to share zoological organization expertise with the inspector. Agency inspectors are generally caring, knowledgeable professionals familiar with the broad-ranging and extensive AWA regulations. There may, however, be instances where zoological organizations or their staff have unique experience or formidable expertise which may help further the inspector's understanding of how particular regulations (especially those which are performance-based) could be applied. Sharing this expertise and engaging in constructive dialogue during the inspection can often be mutually beneficial. This is especially so when there is no pressing concern but where a groundwork of knowledge can be provided about important activities, practices or programs to build awareness for future inspections.

Documenting the Inspection

5.   *Note-taking*

Throughout the inspection, the Animal Welfare Leadership Group should have at least one member taking notes specific to the proceedings, as well as recording other items in need of attention or undergoing improvement at the time of the inspection. This may include taking photographs or video and sound recordings of certain items or activities, such as specific animal behaviors. The Animal Welfare Leadership Group must be fully engaged with the inspector or inspection team during every inspection. Their priority must be listening to the inspector and understanding what he or she is seeing or perceiving. Attentive and respectful engagement makes for more constructive inspections. This helps the zoological organization manifest its commitment to continuous improvement and EXCELLENCE BEYOND COMPLIANCE.

6.   *Photographs*

The Compliance Officer should request copies of photographs taken by the inspector during the inspection (pursuant to the Freedom of Information Act, if necessary) and should take their own photographs (and video and sound recordings) of any items of note, even if they are not formal noncompliant items. Photographs should also be taken of previous noncompliant items that have been corrected, and of other recent improvements. Photographs and recordings should be date- and time-stamped so as to provide an accurate view of conditions during the inspection. Contemporaneous photographic or recorded evidence of conditions observed during and remedied during or subsequent to an inspection is vitally important. Requesting and/or duplicating photographic evidence compiled during an inspection can help alleviate misunderstandings and provide other zoological organization staff with a clear picture depicting conditions, especially those in need of immediate attention or worth recognizing for positive reinforcement.

7.   *Zoological organization records*

Zoological organization records reviewed or copied during an inspection should be clearly identified in the zoological organization's own inspection notes to facilitate more complete self-examination of the inspection. As mentioned with respect to photographic evidence, documentary evidence and records compiled during an inspection should be noted and clearly marked (if not copied) in order to ensure the zoological organization has a clear path as to where to begin any inspection-related review or self-assessment.

Addressing Concerns During Inspections

8.   *Immediately address all concerns whenever possible*

Any and all concerns capable of being addressed and handled immediately, including but not limited to noncompliant items, should be resolved during the inspection (and, if included in the inspection report, noted as "Corrected at the time of inspection"). This is another substantial benefit of having veterinary, buildings and grounds, maintenance, and other staff represented or available during the inspection. Relevant staff can be immediately directed to respond without first reaching out to another departmental manager. Anything and everything corrected or improved during the inspection and before the close of the exit briefing should be photographed, documented, and made available for reinspection or at the exit briefing. At the very least this evidences commitment to continuous compliance and immediate correction or improvement and it may also warrant that any noncompliant item be followed by "Corrected at the time of inspection" on the inspection report—a fact which reinforces good behavior and remains on record. (In some instances the inspector may even have discretion to omit reference to a noncompliance corrected immediately.[30])

9.   *Consult relevant staff*

When time permits during an inspection, prior to an exit briefing, or before the close of an exit briefing, it is often helpful to confer with relevant staff as to any knowledge or understanding they have which might bear upon any items of concern. Reach out to such staff for underlying documentation or their recollection as to anything of potential concern. There may very well be things of which the inspection team is not directly aware. Staff may have invaluable information when asked, and it is usually much more helpful to present any such information during the inspection, and certainly before the close of the exit briefing, than in the course of subsequent proceedings.

10.   *Discuss correction dates for noncompliant items*

Correction dates relating to any noncompliant items should at least be discussed while at the site of the item. Correction dates are critical to AWA compliance, animal welfare, and EXCELLENCE BEYOND COMPLIANCE. To clearly understand what needs to be corrected or fixed and the appropriate time frame for completion, it is best to at least preliminarily discuss correction dates while observing the actual animals or conditions, and with representatives of relevant staff present.

---

[30] See *Animal Welfare Inspection Guide*, General Inspection Procedures, Completing the Inspection Report at 3-26.

V: THE INSPECTION EXIT BRIEFING

Sometimes when I consider what tremendous consequences come from little things I am tempted to think there are no little things.

Bruce Barton

1. *Conduct a formal exit briefing with the inspector*

As stated earlier, being fully engaged with the inspector during the inspection and highly responsive to any concerns and corrections makes for better inspections and better zoological organizations. Exit briefings are a critical component of this process and should be conducted face-to-face at the end of every inspection.

The exit briefing should include review of any noncompliant items and correction dates, and can also be used to seek informal guidance or feedback as to these and other matters (e.g., what may be done to correct a noncompliance). The zoological organization should make certain that it clearly understands what is required. This opportunity should be seized to ask any questions relating to noncompliant items, the wording of the inspection report narrative, and correction dates, as well as to resolve any differences.

At the end of the exit briefing, the written inspection report should be presented for review and signature.[31]

---

[31] The *Animal Welfare Inspection Guide* states at 2-6:

> The signature of the licensee/registrant or his/her representative certifies that the person received a copy of the inspection report. It does not necessarily mean that the person agrees with the findings of the inspection.

2.   *Zoological organization Chief Executive participation in the exit briefing*

If at all possible, it is very helpful to have the zoological organization's Chief Executive present for at least part of the exit briefing. Having a zoological organization's top person involved and wholly supportive of AWA compliance, animal welfare, and EXCELLENCE BEYOND COMPLIANCE is important. When this individual participates in even a portion of an exit briefing it underscores the full extent of organizational commitment.

3.   *Address all corrected items during the exit briefing*

While the exit briefing is being conducted, invite the inspector to revisit any issues addressed and corrected during the inspection (if the inspector has not already observed or re-reviewed the condition[s] or documentation). If the inspector does not have time or is not interested in revisiting the issue in question, present photographs and documentation evidencing the repair or correction. Then request that if any such previously noncompliant item is referenced in the inspection report it be noted as "Corrected at the time of inspection." This allows the inspector and the agency to document compliance history as well as remedial action in the inspection report. It should also reinforce a zoological organization's commitment to moving quickly during and after the inspection to address any concerns, noncompliant items, or enhancements.

4.   *Discuss concerns with relevant staff*

As already noted in Chapter IV: *During an Inspection*, item 9, it can be very helpful to confer with relevant staff during an inspection regarding any areas of concern. If such consultation has not already occurred it should be undertaken prior to the close of the exit briefing. Staff can frequently provide unique insights into specific situations and it is typically most helpful to present inspectors with such information immediately rather than in the course of subsequent proceedings.

5.   *Clarify the process for addressing noncompliant items*

Take stock of all items to be corrected, as well as the correction dates or deadlines, during the exit briefing. The zoological organization should be certain that it understands the manner in which it may correct a noncompliant item as well as the process for verifying and documenting correction of any noncompliances. This is the best opportunity to make certain that relevant officials and staff clearly understand the inspector's concerns, agency requirements, what must actually be done, and the relevant time frames.

6.   *Carefully review the inspection report*

When reviewing the inspection report, keep in mind that all the contents, including wording and regulations cited, can be critical. If the inspection report is not challenged on appeal or otherwise amended it is the final record of compliance and associated conditions at the time of inspection. Sometimes there are different regulations that may be more accurate statements of a noncompliance, or there may be better, more constructive ways to describe a situation. Take great care during the exit briefing to make certain the references, descriptions and wording are accurate and appropriate.

7.   *Ending the exit briefing prior to receiving the inspection report*

There may be rare cases when it may be advisable or necessary to conclude the face-to-face exit briefing without receiving the final inspection report. This may be acceptable if the zoological organization and the inspector are engaged in a constructive dialogue and one or both parties may want to further examine some information shortly after the exit briefing. (Sometimes this review, or a need for review with others in the agency, may lead to an inspection report with a placemarker notation as to a specific item or items being under review.)

8.   *Addressing remaining differences regarding the contents of the inspection report*

If there remain any differences over the final contents or wording of the inspection report, respectfully advise the inspector that the zoological organization may evaluate whether to commence an inspection report appeal relating to such points. The inspection and the exit briefing provide the two best opportunities to resolve any differences between the inspector and the zoological organization. If there are any issues on which the zoological organization still respectfully disagrees at the close of the exit briefing, it is good etiquette to politely advise the inspector that any "open items" will be reviewed and may be the subject of further discussion or, if necessary, an inspection report appeal. This simply gives the inspector a courtesy "heads up" that an item might be subject to further constructive process.

VI: AFTER AN INSPECTION

We must not, in trying to think about how we can make a big difference, ignore the small daily differences we can make which, over time, add up to big differences that we often cannot foresee.

Marian Wright Edelman

1.   Internal debriefing

The AWA Compliance Officer, Animal Welfare Officer, and Animal Welfare Leadership Group should review and discuss the inspection, exit briefing and inspection report as soon as possible. Discussion should consider things that went well during the inspection process, and things the organization could improve upon in subsequent inspections. The substance of the inspection report and follow-up actions should also be discussed (as detailed further below). Even with a clean inspection report, constructive review of the inspection experience may lead to potential enhancements in various areas, including those related to AWA compliance and animal welfare.

Corrective Measures and Improvements

2.   *Address noncompliant items, other concerns and enhancements*

Immediately following the exit briefing, address any noncompliant items and other concerns and develop plans for longer-term actions. Anything directly impacting animal welfare must be given highest priority. Remedial efforts should not be limited to immediate fixes but should also consider additional improvements to avoid repeat occurrences or to incorporate enhancements to animal welfare, including measures not necessarily directly related to the noncompliant item or affected animals.

For example, a noncompliant item relating to the maintenance of an exhibit or housing area could trigger internal review and voluntary actions or upgrades in other similar exhibit or housing areas. It could also prompt other enhancements relating to the affected species, even if such enhancements are unrelated to the specific noncompliant item. This is the very heart of EXCELLENCE BEYOND COMPLIANCE: always do more than what is required, especially as it relates to animal welfare.[32]

3. *Document corrective actions and improvements*

Subsequent to an inspection involving any concerns (which may not have risen to the level of a noncompliant item) or noncompliant items, every correction and improvement should be documented with date- and time-stamped photographs or other records.

4. *Self-certified compliance reporting*

Unless a zoological organization has a compelling reason not to do this, a "self-certified compliance report" should be submitted to Animal Care, through its inspector, as soon as possible. It can be as simple as noting that these conditions have been corrected as of such date and that photographic evidence of corrective measures is on file and can be provided upon reinspection, or it could include all associated documentation. Such submissions could identify the corrected/improved items and contain more formal language like the following, based upon the wording in existing APHIS forms:[33]

---

[32] For those wanting to embark on more systematic improvements, see this chapter, items 16 & 17, and Chapter VII, *Investigations and Enforcement*, item 8.

[33] Adapted from APHIS forms 7003-A (Application for New License) and 7003 (Renewal) (*Appendix A: License Application and Renewal Forms*) based upon the existing regulatory authority in 9 C.F.R. § 2.2(a) and (b).

I make this submission relating to corrective measures [and/or, if applicable, additional enhancements] made under the Animal Welfare Act 7 U.S.C. 2131 et seq. I certify that the information provided herein is true and correct to the best of my knowledge. I hereby acknowledge receipt of and certify to the best of my knowledge _____ is in compliance with all regulations and standards in 9 CFR, Subpart A, Parts 1, 2, and 3. I certify that I am over 18 years of age.

As noted above, for those zoological organizations that prefer to provide more succinct information, a statement could be submitted simply noting that any and all noncompliant items have been corrected, and that the corrections have been documented in a file available upon reinspection or during the next routine inspection. (That file should immediately be provided at the outset of the entrance briefing during the next inspection.)

The zoological organization can request that Animal Care make this report available to those seeking the zoological organization's inspection report. Inspection reports are posted online.[34] They are readily accessible to the world 24/7, and it is better to document compliance in advance of reinspection or the next routine inspection. Otherwise the outside world, including zoological organization supporters, may have an inaccurate view of conditions and of the organization's commitment to animal welfare based upon one fleeting snapshot of time memorialized in an inspection report.

Although the agency uses a risk-based inspection system, based in part on compliance history, it is important to note that self-certified compliance reporting and EXCELLENCE BEYOND COMPLIANCE are not intended to reduce or replace unannounced agency inspections (or reinspections). Rather, EXCELLENCE BEYOND COMPLIANCE is designed to make the most of each inspection so as to foster AWA compliance, enhance animal welfare, validate good work and help zoological organizations continuously improve.

---

[34] See note 18.

5.   *Requesting reinspection*

In some cases, a zoological organization may also want to request an expedited reinspection (or a focused inspection) to obtain confirmation that corrective measures or other improvements are fully compliant and satisfactory to the agency. The inspector may not be able to accommodate such a request, but making it evidences willingness for further external review to validate positive actions.

(Sometimes it may be advisable to invite in an agency species specialist to provide a "courtesy review" of things in order to get the benefit of their guidance based on personal observation. This may be especially helpful in the context of more complicated or serious challenges. See also Chapter III: *Before an Inspection*, item 16.)

6.   *Upon reinspection or next routine inspection*

At the beginning of an inspection or reinspection, be certain that the inspector is provided documentation as to corrective measures and other improvements. If a zoological organization is engaged in self-certified compliance reporting, this information can either be readily available or resubmitted in person. A clean inspection report—"No noncompliances identified this inspection"—may be sufficient to confirm the correction and resolution of prior noncompliant items, or the subsequent inspection report could note, "Previous noncompliant items relating to _____ have been corrected." (Such wording may be helpful in light of recent changes in how the agency determines whether a noncompliance is a "repeat"; i.e., it need not be the identical noncompliance in the same locations with the same animals, nor must it be on consecutive inspections.[35])

7.   *Self-certified compliance and license renewals*

Every license renewal application on APHIS form 7003 contains a required general certification as to compliance. Critics

---

[35] See *Animal Welfare Inspection Guide*, General Inspection Procedures, Completing the Inspection Report at 3-22 to 3-23.

of the existing renewal process have urged APHIS to modify agency policy and practices, as well as the AWA regulations, to prevent the renewal of any license where there are open or outstanding noncompliant items. Given such criticism, it is good practice to provide the required general certification as to compliance, and to further explicitly self-certify compliance with respect to any previous noncompliant items in conjunction with a license renewal. Prompt attention to noncompliances, and self-certified compliance reporting of the correction of noncompliances, in advance of and in connection with license renewals, strengthens the renewal process. It also demonstrates that the zoological organization takes being licensed and regulated seriously.

8.   *Newly discovered information*

        Zoological organizations should consider providing newly discovered information bearing upon inspection report noncompliances and inspection report appeals. Such information, including things like internal reviews, independent analyses, outside research and improvements, may provide helpful insights to the agency in reviewing a given situation and discussing potential resolution.

Inspection Report Appeals

        The Inspection Report Appeal is a mechanism to allow for review and re-examination of inspection reports or selected items, and perhaps for resolution of other differences. If used properly it can be a very effective tool for addressing concerns about an inspection report and its contents, including interpretations of the regulations. It can also be used to constructively address a broader range of matters with the agency.

        The appeal begins with discussing the inspection report with the inspector. Then, if necessary, consult the agency guidelines on inspection report appeals and timely submission of same to the Regional Office.[36] If uncertainty remains as to how to

---

[36] See 1) *Appendix C: Inspection Report Appeals*: *Animal Welfare Inspection*

proceed, immediately contact the Regional Office to inform them of your interest in appealing and to get clear direction on the current process for handling of the appeal. This process is detailed in the *Animal Welfare Inspection Guide* (2013) and in recent agency guidance.[37] As emphasized below, timing is critical; an organization has a maximum of twenty-one days to submit an appeal after receiving the final inspection report. Once this window has closed, the inspection report becomes a part of the organization's permanent record.

9.   *Act fast*

Inspection report appeals must be filed within twenty-one days of the facility receiving the final inspection report. Any appeal received after the twenty-one day period "will be rejected."[38]

Time is of the essence because there is also a twenty-one day lag before inspection reports are posted online. An appeal commenced within that time period should be accompanied by a request that the inspection report not be posted pending the appeal (which is consistent with current agency policy and practice). This can be extremely helpful to a good zoological organization working to improve itself during the appeals process (as it can then focus on creating improvements).

The appeal process is discussed below; requirements for filing the appeal are detailed more fully in agency guidance.[39]

Guide, General Inspection Procedures, Completing the Inspection Report, Inspection Appeals Process, available at:
http://www.aphis.usda.gov/animal_welfare/downloads/Animal%20Care%20Ins pection%20Guide.pdf, (3-27 to 3-29), and 2) APHIS, Animal Care, Factsheet, Appeals Process (July 2014), available at:
http://www.aphis.usda.gov/publications/animal_welfare/2014/appeals_process.pdf
[37] See *Appendix C: Inspection Report Appeals*.
[38] See *Appendix C: Inspection Report Appeals*, APHIS, Animal Care, Factsheet, Appeals Process (July 2014).
[39] See *Appendix C: Inspection Report Appeals*.

10.   Stay constructive during the appeal

While it may be "good" to "prevail" on appeal, the process is most effective when approached constructively. This allows the zoological organization and the agency to develop enhanced understanding of the AWA and related animal-welfare implications, which can forge more effective inspections and compliance efforts. In other words, an appeal can and should be used to build better working relationships in addition to clarifying and resolving any disputed items.

11.   Make the appeal credible and substantial

Ensure that the inspection report appeal is credible and substantial. A respectfully-submitted appeal (or discussions relating to same) should be focused and to the point, and should present all relevant zoological organization expertise, documentation, professional and scientific literature, agency regulatory history and other guidance. An appeal may also include acknowledgment of where the zoological organization could have done an even better job in explaining a situation or providing all relevant documentation.

12.   Potential bases for appeal

An inspection report appeal can seek review of whether a noncompliant item was really compliant, whether it was a direct or repeat noncompliance, and whether it was corrected at the time of inspection. It can also question or seek to clarify or revise the wording of the inspection report, the proposed correction dates, and whether a noncompliant item was cited under the proper regulatory provision. All of these elements have different consequences for the organization (as well as for animals) and become a permanent part of the organization's compliance history.[40]

---

[40] See also Chapter V: *The Inspection Exit Briefing,* item 6, regarding the relevance of specific wording in inspection reports.

13.   *Outside consultation or review*

Outside consultation or review can prove invaluable during the appeals process. This is the case whether an organization is seeking guidance from the relevant TAG, an expert, consultant or even counsel. Such outside consultation is sought in many situations, not just during inspection report appeals. Independent review and examination may prompt new and different perspectives essential to furthering elevated organizational awareness of and commitment to animal welfare, as well as providing information that is useful on appeal. Sometimes it can even help a zoological organization discover beneficial yet overlooked elements of its own expertise or history. It can also point the way towards additional improvements or research to better assess and ultimately enhance animal welfare.

14.   *Inspection reports, inspection report appeals, and the Freedom of Information Act*

It is important to understand the relationship between inspection reports, inspection report appeals, and the federal Freedom of Information Act (FOIA).[41] Note that in 2012 Animal Care changed its policy and practice with respect to inspection reports, inspection report appeals and FOIA. While inspection reports under appeal are still withheld from disclosure online, hard copies are available pursuant to a FOIA request. In the event an inspection report under appeal is disclosed pursuant to a FOIA request, be prepared to use the following agency statements and, if necessary, request confirmation of these agency positions from the appropriate Regional Office to make clear the subject inspection report is non-final.

> An inspection report may be amended to correct an error or in response to an appeal submitted by a USDA licensee/registrant.

* * *

---

[41] The Freedom of Information Act, 5 U.S.C. § 552, available at: http://www.justice.gov/oip/foia_updates/Vol_XVII_4/page2.htm

Once amended, the original, unmodified report is no longer valid, and the revised report becomes the final determination of compliance by APHIS.[42]

Beyond the Appeal

15.   Do not rely on a successful appeal

EXCELLENCE BEYOND COMPLIANCE is about constructive action and continuous improvement. A zoological organization committed to EXCELLENCE BEYOND COMPLIANCE will not depend on a successful appeal but will also, where appropriate and practical, immediately seek to address underlying concerns and consider additional improvements. Thus, whether an appeal ultimately succeeds or falls short, the zoological organization will have used the time during which the appeal is pending to make advances which transform previous issues into valuable lessons towards enhancing animal welfare and advancing excellence.

16.   ZIPs, AIPs, PIPs and Animal Welfare Enhancement Plans

Zoological organizations should always be working off of an intermediate or long range strategic plan (including an Animal Welfare Plan). However, in the event of serious incidents and/or compliance challenges, or simply to jumpstart an animal welfare initiative, Zoo, Aquarium or Park Improvement Plans (ZIPs, AIPs or PIPs) or Animal Welfare Enhancement Plans (for a specific species) should also be developed. EXCELLENCE BEYOND COMPLIANCE requires more than simply fixing problems and moving on. Problem resolution is the starting point. Challenges are constructively examined for the lessons they bring, with the goals of continuous improvement, animal welfare enhancements and advancement of organizational excellence. Consideration should therefore be given to remedying and preventing recurrence of

---

[42] Animal Care Letter to Stakeholders, *Update from Chester Gipson, Animal Care Deputy Administrator regarding the posting of amended versus original inspection reports on APHIS' website* (2012). See note 36, *Appendix C*.

noncompliances as well as to promoting additional animal welfare-related enhancements.

17.   *Key elements of effective improvement and enhancement plans*

Effective and successful ZIPs, AIPs, PIPs and Animal Welfare Enhancement Plans generally contain certain foundational elements. Part of the process involved in creating such plans might include doing a needs assessment based on current conditions. All plans should evaluate and consider improvements relating to: staffing (numbers, allocation, experience and expertise); training (staff and animal training levels and programs); veterinary care; facilities (condition, maintenance, surface renewal, monitoring, and, longer-term, how well they serve animal needs, including in some instances recognizing the need for expanded or new facilities); and communication (including inter-departmental cooperation and instructions to the public); recordkeeping and research.

The best improvement and enhancement plans are "living documents" which establish a new baseline and are continuously improved upon and periodically updated. Preparation and implementation of improvement and enhancement plans can be a tremendous force for good. Improving and updating them is truly EXCELLENCE BEYOND COMPLIANCE.

VII: INVESTIGATIONS AND ENFORCEMENT

Every adversity, every failure, every heartache carries with it the seed of an equal or greater benefit.

Napoleon Hill

It is vital for any organization facing the challenge of an investigation to immediately retain counsel. The discussion in this chapter should in no way supersede the advice of, or mitigate the need for, appropriate legal counsel. It is merely illustrative of how the principles of EXCELLENCE BEYOND COMPLIANCE can help support an organization that is the subject of an investigation. Subject to consultation with counsel, a zoological organization committed to EXCELLENCE BEYOND COMPLIANCE should remain constructive and continuously dedicated to improvement (especially animal-related enhancements) even while it is involved in these types of situations.

Investigations

Even fine zoological organizations may find themselves in the enforcement process where Investigative Enforcement Services (IES) will get involved in working with Animal Care to investigate a case. This could be the result of an unfortunate high profile incident or tragedy, an inspection report or reports with serious, direct noncompliant items, and/or evidence of a pattern of noncompliance. It may also arise from a complaint.

If an organization knows or has reason to believe that it is the subject of an investigation, it is strongly recommended that the organization make constructive use of this situation while properly protecting itself.

1. Seeking counsel

Zoological organizations dealing with serious incidents and potential or actual investigations should immediately seek counsel as needed. This counsel can come from knowledgeable accrediting and other professional associations in which the organization participates, and should likely also include legal and public relations counsel to make certain that while being proactive and pursuing the truth (which is critical), the organization's legal rights and reputational interests are protected. This is especially important if there are other substantial third-party interests involved relating to employees or the public. In addition to appropriate expertise, counsel should also always demonstrate sensitivity to the animal-related considerations inherent in the situation.

2. Preparedness for an investigation

Once a zoological organization is subject to an investigation (or when it is aware it will likely undergo one), it should be better prepared and more knowledgeable about the situation than any other individual, group or organization. An APHIS investigation and potential enforcement action are extremely serious matters. Ill-prepared organizations compound any underlying problems, leave themselves unprotected, and may appear to fail to appropriately demonstrate concern for animals, staff and the public. Well-prepared organizations seek to develop an understanding of all the facts so as to assess what, if anything, went wrong, why, and how it should be addressed. To the best of their ability, well-prepared organizations accept accountability as appropriate and work to resolve challenges. Simply put, they do more to make things better instead of waiting for agency action (though such organizations are mindful of agency processes and the implications thereof, and will certainly adjust their approach accordingly as needed and in consultation with counsel).

3.   Understanding the investigative/enforcement process

Understanding how the agency, especially IES, handles the investigation and enforcement process is essential. There is ample information on the agency website and in related publications.[43] IES itself has set out the steps in the process as follows:

Investigative Process:

- When APHIS personnel discover a potential violation of APHIS regulations, they may request a formal investigation by IES.
- The investigation is a fact finding mission, which may include collecting documents; taking photographs; and interviewing witnesses, including the alleged violator.
- As part of its investigative process, IES provides alleged violators with the opportunity to submit any evidence that may clear them of wrongdoing.
- Once the investigation is complete, the Investigator prepares a ROI [Report of Investigation], which summarizes the investigative findings.
- The Investigator sends the ROI and all evidence collected to IES' enforcement staff for review.

Enforcement Process:

- When the enforcement staff receives the ROI and accompanying evidence, a Specialist reviews and analyzes this information to determine if the violation is substantiated by the evidence provided.

---

[43] See note 7, *Appendix F:* including, 1) IES Frequently Asked Questions, available at: http://www.aphis.usda.gov/wps/portal/aphis/resources/enforcement-actions?1dmy&urile=wcm%3apath%3a%2Faphis_content_library%2Fsa_our_f ocus%2Fsa_business_services%2Fsa_mrpbs_divisions%2Fsa_ies%2Fct_ies_faq 2) Open Letter to Stakeholders on Investigation and Enforcement Process Streamlining (January 2012), available at: http://www.aphis.usda.gov/ies/pdf/ies_stakeholders_letter.pdf and 3) APHIS, Investigative and Enforcement Services, Factsheet, *Questions and Answers: APHIS Enforcement Process Streamlining* (January 2012), available at: http://www.aphis.usda.gov/publications/aphis_general/2012/IES_process.pdf

- If the evidence shows a violation occurred, the enforcement staff determines whether an enforcement action is appropriate.
- What enforcement action is taken, if any, depends on the seriousness of the issue and the number of alleged violations, among other things.
- Before carrying out any enforcement action, IES consults with the referring program [i.e., Animal Care for the AWA].
- Enforcement actions may include an official warning, a voluntary settlement agreement, a referral to the Office of the General Counsel (OGC) for administrative action, or, in cases involving the most serious violations, a referral to the United States Department of Justice for civil or criminal action.
- When IES issues an official warning, it closes the investigative file involving the alleged violation.
- Pre-litigation settlement agreements.
  - In appropriate instances, IES may offer pre-litigation settlement agreements to alleged violators. These settlement agreements may include a monetary penalty or other sanction. IES determines monetary penalties using guidelines that APHIS developed based on penalty provisions in the various laws that APHIS administers.
  - Settlement agreements generally contain settlement terms that are more favorable to the alleged violator than what APHIS would seek through administrative, civil, or criminal action.
  - Settlement agreements advise the alleged violator that he or she has an opportunity for a hearing, and that he or she may waive the hearing by accepting the settlement agreement and paying the penalty (or accepting the terms of settlement) within a specified time.
  - If the alleged violator accepts the settlement agreement, IES closes its investigative file.
  - If the alleged violator does not accept the settlement agreement, IES will refer the violation to OGC for administrative action,

generally seeking a larger penalty or more serious sanction.

- IES may also refer a violation directly to OGC for administrative action, without first offering a settlement agreement.
- The Rules of Practice[44] Applicable to Proceedings Pending Before the Secretary of Agriculture govern all proceedings filed by OGC.[45]

This overview of the investigation and enforcement process from the IES webpages is a "must read" if an investigation is likely.

4.   "High-priority" designation cases

APHIS Animal Care, in conjunction with IES, may give certain cases a "high-priority" designation, which means that they will be expedited through the investigative and enforcement process. The agency uses the "high-priority" designation on cases based on the following criteria:

- Severity of animal suffering (death or severe injury),
- Past compliance history of facility,
- Potential public or animal safety or health concerns,
- Abusive or potentially violent nature of licensee or registrant,
- Type of facility and species of animal involved, and;
- Severity of the issue resulting in extensive public interest.[46]

---

[44] See *USDA Rules of Practice Governing Formal Adjudicatory Administrative Proceedings Instituted by the Secretary* (Compiled April 20, 2005), available at: http://www.dm.usda.gov/oaljdecisions/RulesofPractice.pdf

[45] See 1) AWA Enforcement Home Page (defining and providing links for types of enforcement actions), available at: http://www.aphis.usda.gov/wps/portal/aphis/ourfocus/animalwelfare?1dmy&urile=wcm%3apath%3a%2Faphis_content_library%2Fsa_our_focus%2Fsa_animal_welfare%2Fsa_awa%2Fct_awa_enforcements and 2) Investigative and Enforcement Services (IES) Home Page (detailing "Investigative Process" and "Enforcement Process" and providing additional information), available at: http://www.aphis.usda.gov/wps/portal/aphis/resources/ enforcement-actions

[46] See note 45, AWA Enforcement Home Page (The High-Priority Designation).

5.   *Potential "ground rules" for dealing with investigations*

Zoological organizations dealing with serious incidents and potential or actual investigations should, in consultation with counsel, establish reasonable "ground rules" for dealing with any such investigations. The organization's leadership and staff are required to be truthful and are best served by being cooperative with the agency (even while exercising the right to counsel). Nevertheless, it is appropriate to mutually establish reasonable ground rules for the conduct of the investigation. These should including the following:

- Staff availability should be managed with regard for staff responsibilities (e.g., interviews will be held at times staff is not needed to fulfill essential animal welfare functions).
- If counsel is unable to attend interviews (or as a reasonable accommodation to conserve zoological organization resources for animal welfare), a management-level staff person should be allowed to sit in on all interviews (counsel should, however, be available via telephone if needed).
- Any draft sworn statements prepared by the agency that are based on staff interviews should be reviewed by counsel prior to staff signing of the sworn statement.
- Copies of all documentary or other evidence and records taken by the investigator should be identified and copied (or marked for ease of internal review).

6.   *Upon the conclusion of an investigation*

Once IES has finished its investigation (and consulted with Animal Care) a case is usually either closed or a proposed settlement or complaint is issued. There is no formal mechanism for requiring that a zoological organization be informed that a case has been closed, but inquiries can certainly be made to ascertain whether a matter is closed or pending. It is in the best interests of animal welfare and the zoological organization to follow through with the agency in order to remain updated on the status of a case and to ensure compliance and/or appropriate follow-up action, including potential enhancements.

Settlement

7.   *Settlement via stipulation*

Settlement via stipulation (prior to a hearing) or consent decree (after a hearing; see next section below: *Defending the Prosecution of Alleged Noncompliant Items*) can be an effective step in moving forward. Reasonable settlement can conserve resources which might instead be invested in activities and enhancements directly benefiting animals. Appropriate settlement can also preclude adverse adjudication or findings on the merits (perhaps establishing culpability), preserve reputational integrity (if approached constructively and proactively), and serve to establish a fresh starting point for continuous AWA compliance. Payment of a civil penalty and avoiding an admission of any noncompliances or alleged or apparent violations may be seen as helpful to a zoological organization. Note, however, that this is merely a starting point for zoological organizations committed to EXCELLENCE BEYOND COMPLIANCE.

8.   *Additional constructive and proactive measures upon and following settlement*

Effective and meaningful settlements of alleged noncompliances or alleged or apparent violations should be accompanied by additional constructive and proactive measures. Zoological organizations committed to EXCELLENCE BEYOND COMPLIANCE (or those deciding to so commit themselves) should do the following prior to settlement:

- Consider and implement all reasonable and necessary measures to prevent reoccurrence of any alleged noncompliant items.
- Consider and implement additional measures to enhance animal welfare (including some not necessarily related to the alleged noncompliant items).
- Develop an Animal Welfare Enhancement Plan or a form of improvement plan in consultation with the agency for

any measures requiring longer-term examination, funding or implementation.

- To the extent possible, invite agency review or inspection to validate and verify zoological organization implementation of reported improvements.

This additional effort puts the animals and the zoological organization in a much better position by the time a settlement is finalized and made public. It makes the settlement the springboard for constructive action to enhance animal welfare.

Defending the Prosecution of Alleged Noncompliant Items

As noted above, an organization may choose to reject a pre-litigation offer of settlement from the agency and invoke its right to a hearing. Another possibility is that IES may not offer a pre-litigation settlement and instead may refer the matter to OGC, which then serves a formal complaint. In such cases, although settlement by consent decree may still be a possibility down the road, the following considerations should be taken into account.

9.   *Invoking the right to a hearing*

If an organization has not yet been served a formal complaint and has a choice as to whether or not to reject a pre-litigation settlement, it should think long and hard about invoking the right to a hearing. This action (in essence demanding a formal complaint and prosecution) constitutes a very serious decision requiring careful consultation with counsel as to the merits of any defense. In some cases a vigorous defense may be necessary and likely to succeed. In many cases, whatever the outcome, the cost in financial terms (i.e., counsel fees and staff time) and reputational damage via added publicity attendant upon adversarial proceedings is often greater than the benefits of proceeding even if a zoological organization ultimately prevails. (Of course, the terms of any potential resolution or settlement must also be weighed in the decision-making process regarding invoking the right to a hearing.)

10.   Going to hearing

Because of the extraordinary challenges involved with going to hearing, should a zoological organization find itself in such circumstances it is essential that it have outstanding defense (litigation) and public relations counsel on its team. This requires substantial resources and provides another reason to carefully weigh this option against the potential consequences, as well as the possibility that a settlement will ultimately conserve greater resources which can be allocated towards enhancing animal welfare.

11.   Expert witness testimony

If the matter calls for expert testimony, a credible and outstanding expert can make a significant difference.[47] Involving an expert witness may also provide the additional benefit of helpful insight into existing conditions that can then be used to better inform enhancements in animal welfare.

12.   Moving forward after a hearing

Whatever the outcome of a hearing—even if a zoological organization prevails, and especially if it does not—it is in the best interests of the organization and the animals in its care to further strengthen its focus on efforts to foster AWA compliance and enhance animal welfare. In short, there is no better practice for zoological organizations to use to protect themselves (and the animals they exist to serve) than to do their very best for the animals entrusted to their care.

---

[47] See, e.g., Hodgins v. U.S. Department of Agriculture, 2000 WL 1785733 (6th Cir. Nov. 29, 2000), aff'd, 33 Fed. Appx. 784, 2002 WL 649102 (6th Cir. Apr. 17, 2002). See also In Re Michael A. Huchital, Ph.D., 58 Agric. Dec. 763, 788 (Nov. 4, 1999) (testimony of expert with substantial animal handling experience accorded greater weight than experienced veterinarians not necessarily familiar with species or handling technique at issue).

VIII: SELECT MATTERS WARRANTING SPECIAL CONSIDERATION

One is not exposed to danger who, even when in safety is always on their guard.

Publilius Syrus

While it is impossible to cover every potential contingency that might occur under the AWA, it is worth noting some critical considerations and special situations in relation to EXCELLENCE BEYOND COMPLIANCE. More complete understanding of these items can be used to foster AWA compliance, enhance animal welfare and advance organizational excellence.

Veterinary Care

1. *Authority of the Attending Veterinarian*

As detailed in the AWA regulations,[48] the attending veterinarian has a critical role in maintaining AWA compliance and animal health, as well as in enhancing animal welfare. Key issues to proactively address include reviewing veterinary authority and establishing a clear path of communication between frontline caregivers and the veterinary staff. The attending veterinarian must have adequate authority to oversee the program

---

[48] See 9 C.F.R. § 2.33 (research facilities) and § 2.40 (exhibitors like zoological organizations). See also *Animal Welfare Inspection Guide* at 6-1 to 6-14 (noting items requiring veterinary consultation as well as those requiring veterinary approval). When the attending veterinarian is part-time or a consultant, a formal written program of veterinary care is required.

of veterinary care and discharge their significant duties under the AWA, which include, but are not limited to, those set forth in the regulations and detailed in the *Animal Welfare Inspection Guide* under "Attending Veterinarian." This has generally been applied to mean that veterinary decisions or judgments must be made by the attending veterinarian rather than by management or caregiving, non-veterinary staff. In some zoological organizations there may be extensive discussion of animal health and treatment amongst key staff. This may even extend to engaging in a somewhat collaborative decision-making process. That judicious deliberation is wonderful, but to the extent that veterinary judgment is involved the agency looks to see "that the attending veterinarian has appropriate authority to ensure the provision of adequate veterinary care and to oversee the adequacy of other aspects of animal care and use."[49]

2.   *Observation and monitoring of animals, and
      communications regarding veterinary treatment*

While lab test results and other data play an important role in veterinary diagnostics, there is no substitute for monitoring, observing, and visually (and, as appropriate, physically) examining animals. Veterinarians may regularly observe animals undergoing treatment, but the attending veterinarian is generally not able to do this with every animal on a daily basis (because of the number of animals or because the veterinarian is offsite). The regulations provide that "daily observation of all animals to assess their health and well-being"[50] may be done by other staff. The regulations also require that "a mechanism of direct and frequent communication is required so that timely and accurate information on problems of animal health, behavior and well-being is conveyed to the attending veterinarian."[51]

To enhance the protection of animal health and welfare, it is essential that relevant caregiving staff appropriately observe and monitor all animals daily. This is a function of experience,

---

[49] See 9 C.F.R. § 2.33(a)(2) and § 2.40(a)(2). See also *Animal Welfare Inspection Guide* at 6-1 to 6-14.
[50] 9 C.F.R. § 2.33(b)(3) and § 2.40(b)(3).
[51] 9 C.F.R. § 2.33(b)(3) and § 2.40(b)(3).

expertise and training. It can be more challenging with larger groups of animals, and in more expansive and naturalistic environments. Measures should be taken to make certain that at least one staff member is clearly accountable for such observations on a given day. Additionally, a clear protocol should be in place for communicating relevant observations to the veterinarian in a timely manner, as well as for ensuring that veterinary instructions are faithfully administered by responsible staff. Communications and recordkeeping systems that make clear any known acute conditions and the status of prescribed treatments are essential for maintaining consistency and continuity among caregiving staff. In addition, systems should be in place to make all veterinary and caregiving staff aware of chronic or recurring conditions which may warrant heightened monitoring and observation at regular intervals.

Animal Handling and Public Safety

3.   *Animal behavior/husbandry/training and animal welfare*

Animal behaviorists and their expertise in understanding animal behavior are a critical part of the animal welfare team. The more expertise brought to bear on observing and understanding animal behavior and empowering animals to engage in natural behaviors, the more effective the animal welfare effort.

In conjunction with advanced understanding of animal behavior, another important tool for facilitating animal welfare, and a key component of "animal handling," is ensuring appropriate training of resident animals through operant conditioning. Good behavioral training aids in voluntary animal participation in husbandry and veterinary examinations and procedures and can be used by staff to help animals become more comfortable with changes in environment, social group or other situations, as well as facilitating the provision of enrichment and exercise.

4. The "general handling" regulation

Under the AWA regulations, "handling" is defined to include almost anything that involves an animal.[52] The "general handling" regulation covers handling of all regulated animals, as well as specific types of handling like public exhibition (including exhibition of dangerous animals), rest for performing animals, exhibition of young animals, public contact, public feeding, public handling, and handling generally.[53] This regulation also requires that staff have species-specific experience and knowledge, as well as measures in place that can be taken to alleviate threats to animal health or well-being due to climatic conditions.[54]

Given the breadth of what "handling" includes and the extent of the "general handling" regulation, the requirements of this section are of increasing importance with respect to AWA compliance and enhancing animal welfare. It is also the cornerstone of addressing public safety under the AWA.

5. Public safety and animal welfare

The AWA is meant to protect covered animals by ensuring they are afforded humane care and treatment. An important, sometimes underappreciated (even by this author some years ago) element of this protection relates to public safety. Simply put, public safety is a significant consideration potentially impacting animal welfare. As Chief Judge Posner noted in Hoctor v. United States Department of Agriculture (a big cat containment case), though the purpose of the AWA is to protect animals, "if one of those Cats mauled or threatened a human being, the Cat might get into serious trouble and thus *it is necessary to protect the human*

---

[52] 9 C.F.R. § 1.1 defines "handling" as "petting, feeding, watering, cleaning, manipulating, loading, crating, shifting, transferring, immobilizing, restraining, treating, training, working and moving, or any similar activity with respect to any animal."

[53] 9 C.F.R. § 2.131 (b), (c) and (d). For detailed guidance on what the agency looks for in certain public contact and exhibition situations see *Animal Welfare Inspection Guide* at Animal Rides 4-6, Drive-Through Zoo 4-23, Petting Zoo 4-31, and Photo Shoot 4-36.

[54] 9 C.F.R. § 2.131 (a) and (e).

beings from Big Cats, in order to protect the Cats from human beings, which is the important thing under the Act."[55]

The regulations relating to safety include, without limitation, the general handling regulation (especially handling "so there is minimal risk of harm to the animal and the public, with sufficient distance and/or barriers between the animals and the general viewing public to assure the safety of the animals and the public"[56]) as well as regulations relating to facilities that require they be constructed and maintained in good repair to securely contain the animals.[57]

Because safety, including public, employee and inspector safety, can impact AWA compliance and animal welfare, it is extremely helpful to include a Safety Officer in the compliance effort and in the Animal Welfare Leadership Group (as mentioned above in Chapter II: *Organizational Framework,* item 5).

6.   Public interaction with animals

Safe handling of animals is especially important during times of public contact or interaction, such as in petting zoos or special-event situations. In such cases it is imperative for animal and public safety to have dedicated and experienced animal-handling or training staff present to focus primarily on the animals. Additional training, handling or, better yet, other staff should be employed to guide and monitor the public, especially when the public is not directly engaged with animal interactions. This frees up qualified animal handlers and trainers to focus exclusive attention on the animals in their care. Furthermore, zoological organization security staff should be keenly aware of the time and place of interactive or public contact areas and events so as to be

---

[55] Hoctor v. United States Department of Agriculture, 82 F.3d 165, 168-169 (7th Cir. 1996) (emphasis added).

[56] 9 C.F.R. § 2.131(b)(1).

[57] See, e.g., 9 C.F.R. § 3.75(a) (nonhuman primates), 9 C.F.R. § 3.101(a) (marine mammals) and 9 C.F.R. § 3.125(a) (other warm-blooded animals). These are simply the most obvious safety-related regulations. Regulations relating to enclosure features and size, materials and surfaces, drainage, social grouping, training, veterinary care, recordkeeping and other factors can all have animal and human (public, staff and inspector) safety implications.

better prepared for any contingency that may impact them, including the possibility of a facility-wide emergency unrelated to the interaction or public contact.

These considerations highlight the potential benefit of cross training zoological organization staff, including those responsible for animal-handling, training, safety and security.

7.   Special circumstances and events

There are situations (e.g., construction, major renovation, substantial maintenance operations like tree-trimming) and special events (e.g., VIP and large after-hours social programs), in which animals may be subjected to potentially disruptive conditions to which they are not acclimated. During the planning for such activities, animal caregiving staff should be fully engaged to advise on any particular animal sensitivities and to develop and recommend precautions to better protect potentially-affected animals (e.g., creating "buffer areas" or "safe zones" that minimize or even eliminate any impact). Additionally, while the actual work or event is underway it is recommended that an Animal Welfare Monitor be utilized to monitor the activities and the animals. This individual should have the authority to direct corrective or protective action, should it become necessary. Observations and insights gained during these activities can then be used to inform and improve processes, including animal and staff training, and to further mitigate the potential impact of future construction and other activities.

8.   Contingency plans

One of the most effective means for protecting animals and for providing for public safety is the preparation of contingency plans and the implementation of related measures, including training. In 2012, the agency issued a final rule requiring contingency plans and then subsequently temporarily stayed the regulation.[58] Although the regulation remains stayed as of this

---

[58] 9 C.F.R. § 2.134 (temporarily stayed, 78 Fed. Reg. 46255 (July 31, 2013)). See also APHIS Animal Care Final Rule on Handling of Animals, Contingency Plans, 77 Fed. Reg. 76815 (Dec. 31, 2012), available at: http://www.aphis.

writing, it is anticipated that the stay of the regulation will eventually be lifted and the substantive requirements of the regulation will remain largely unchanged. As the temporarily-stayed regulation contains much helpful guidance to avoid and mitigate various emergency scenarios, key components are noted here as things zoological organizations "should" do— whereas if the regulation were in effect they would be requirements.[59] To promote animal welfare through enhanced awareness of potential disaster, emergency and similar scenarios, and to assist in preparation for such situations, zoological organizations should identify, plan, prepare and train for a variety of contingencies. These efforts should be documented and current for all staff. Zoological organizations should identify the particular disasters, emergencies and other situations they are likely to experience and then plan accordingly to provide for the welfare of animals, staff and the public in those situations. Preparation includes creating a detailed outline of specific tasks, establishing a clear chain of command, training of responsible staff, ensuring availability of necessary equipment and materials and backup systems, and finally the documentation and review of all these elements.[60] It is also essential to coordinate planning and training (or cross training) with all appropriate emergency services agencies and first responders.

---

usda.gov/animal_welfare/content/printable_version/contingency_rule_docket.pdf
[59] See *Appendix D: Contingency Plans*, including 1) USDA, APHIS, Animal Care Tech Note, *Considerations When Making a Contingency Plan*, December 2012, available at: http://www.aphis.usda.gov/animal_welfare/content/printable_version/contingency_rule_tech.pdf and 2) APHIS, Animal Care, Factsheet *Questions and Answers: Final Rule on Contingency Plans for Regulated Entities*, January 2013, available at: http://www.aphis.usda.gov/animal_welfare/content/printable_version/contingency_rule_faq.pdf
[60] See note 59, *Appendix D*. See also 1) "Information resources for Institutional Animal Care and Use Committees 1985-1999: Disaster Planning for Animal Facilities," available at: http://www.nal.usda.gov/awic/pubs/IACUC/dis.htm#disainformation and 2) "Zoo Best Practices Working Group," available at: http://www.zooanimalhealthnetwork.org/zoobest.aspx

Animal Transport and Introduction

The transport of animals is a regular occurrence and it comes about for a variety of reasons, including breeding (which is vitally important with respect to endangered species), inclusion in new and/or more compatible social groups, and special care needs. Depending upon the characteristics of the animal and species, transports require great—at the very least—and often extraordinary care, as well as formal plans for introduction of the animal to its new environment. There are many components to a successful transport and introduction which ensure the well-being of the animals (and their handlers) whether in transit or before and after they are transported.

9.   *Transport plans*

Although AWA regulations only require veterinarian-approved transport plans for marine mammal transports greater than two hours,[61] such plans are enormously helpful in safeguarding *all* animals during transportation. Information generally included in transport plans consists of details like the means of transport, travel containers, route, accompanying staff, care, handling, monitoring and data-recording instructions, ambient temperature parameters, provision of adequate ventilation and air circulation, contingency plans and emergency contacts and facilities along the route.

10.   *Letter of veterinary accompaniment*

The marine mammal regulations also require that plans for transports over two hours specify whether it is necessary for a veterinarian to be present during the transport.[62] This requirement makes certain that the attending veterinarian considers carefully whether a veterinarian should travel with the animal. The attending veterinarian then records their determination and the reasons for it

---

[61] 9 C.F.R. § 3.116(a). Significantly, this language emanates from the consensus language agreed upon by all stakeholders during the Marine Mammal Negotiated Rulemaking. See below, note 83.
[62] 9 C.F.R. § 3.116(a).

in writing, either in the transport plan or in a separate letter of veterinary accompaniment. Such deliberate consideration of a key animal health protective factor makes sense, and its application could be broadened to be used for other animal transports, not just those involving marine mammals.

11.   Pre-transport training

Properly preparing an animal (and accompanying staff) for transport is absolutely critical to safe and successful animal movements. In most cases, to the extent possible, acclimation to all aspects of the loading and crating process is important to make an animal more comfortable at the beginning of the transport process as well as while in transit. A pre-transit training plan and adequate time for implementation are essential.

12.   Introduction plans

Upon an animal's arrival at a new zoological organization and following any required quarantine, the animal will be introduced to a new facility and often to another animal or new social group. To ensure proper handling of both the new animal and any other animals currently at the facility, well-thought-out introduction plans should be in place. To maintain and enhance animal welfare, introduction plans should take into account the characteristics of each animal and social group involved, and should be collaboratively developed and implemented. Key elements in successful introductions include understanding the unique personalities and relationships of the animals and their prior introduction experiences, staff monitoring, recordkeeping and ongoing review and discussion of the situation. Consultations with staff at the originating organization and with the relevant TAG or SSP can be of great assistance. Furthermore, it can be extremely helpful to have staff from the receiving zoological organization spend time with the animal and staff at the originating zoological organization pre-transport, and then to have staff from the originating zoological organization spend time with the animal and staff at the receiving zoological organization post-transport.

Serious Incidents

13.   Self-reporting serious incidents

Zoological organizations dealing with serious incidents (and potential or actual investigations) should self-report any serious incidents to APHIS. In doing so they should be especially mindful of agency statements about such situations. The agency has noted the following:

> An incident or adverse event is an occurrence that includes but is not limited to:
>
> - Facility disasters, such as floods or fires;
> - Mishandling or escapes;
> - Attacks and fighting between animals as a result of incompatibility;
> - Human injury as a result of an animal attack;
> - Injury or death related to cage washers, environmental enrichment devices, and squeeze or guillotine mechanisms; and,
> - Failures in HVAC systems, automatic feeders, or watering systems.[63]

There is no regulatory requirement that AWA licensees or registrants report incidents or adverse events to APHIS Animal Care, with the exception of an event that results in the suspension of certain activities at a research facility.[64] Licensees and registrants may choose to report incidents or adverse events in order to advise Animal Care of the situation, provide

---

[63] See *Appendix E: Serious Incidents:* 1) APHIS, Animal Care, Stakeholders Announcement, *Inspection Procedures in Response to an Incident or Adverse Event in Regulated Facilities* (May 11, 2012), available at:
http://www.aphis.usda.gov/publications/animal_welfare/2012/inspection_incide nt_response_sa.pdf and 2) Factsheet, *Questions and Answers: Inspection Procedures in Response to an Incident or Adverse Event* (May 2012), available at: http://www.aphis.usda.gov/publications/animal_welfare/2012/inspection_incide nt_response_faq.pdf
[64] See 9 C.F.R. § 2.31(d)(7).

documentation of their corrective actions, or demonstrate their good faith intention to comply with the AWA and regulations.

Even if self-reporting is not required in a given situation, it is generally better practice to self-report to the agency. Self-reporting may also allow the zoological organization to immediately avail itself of agency expertise or resources in addressing the situation. It also ensures that the agency is quickly informed (rather than subsequently embarrassed when hearing about things from the media or a third party). Furthermore, it underscores the importance the zoological organization places on immediate disclosure and internal review of difficult situations. In a sense, it forces a zoological organization to be more proactive and rigorous in its examination and review of incidents.

14. Prompt "good faith" action

The agency has indicated that it will take into account prompt good faith action (presumably involving self-reporting), particularly when the following factors are present:

- The licensee/registrant found the problem in a timely manner.
- The incident or adverse event was not reasonably foreseeable.
- Timely and appropriate corrective action was taken to prevent a recurrence.
- There is no ongoing pattern of violations at the facility, and
- There were no serious animal welfare impacts.[65]

15. Avoiding speculation

Zoological organizations self-reporting serious incidents should not speculate unduly about things which are uncertain. While it may be helpful to imagine or suggest how things may have happened, premature or excessive speculation may create

---

[65] See note 63, *Appendix E*: APHIS, Animal Care, Stakeholders Announcement, *Inspection Procedures in Response to an Incident or Adverse Event in Regulated Facilities*, (May 11, 2012), available at: http://www.aphis.usda. gov/publications/animal_welfare/2012/inspection_incident_response_sa.pdf

confusion and complicate an appropriate, better-informed resolution. It is advisable to avoid speculation until the zoological organization has obtained as much information as possible.

16.   Internal review of serious incidents

Zoological organizations dealing with serious incidents (and potential or actual investigations) should commence their own internal review. Based on the findings of this review, and after consultation with counsel, they should then present appropriate information, including corrective measures and other potential improvements, to the agency. Immediate and thorough internal review in such cases is obviously important preparation for a zoological organization, both for investigations and, if needed, for its defense. More importantly, earnest internal review and self-examination can lead to a greater understanding of potential causal factors and the development and implementation of responsive improvements and enhancements beyond those necessary to avoid a repeat of the incident. Constructive measures considered and/or implemented should be reported to the agency to impress upon them and others the unyielding organizational commitment to constantly improving animal welfare. (The exact handling and presentation of such measures should be reviewed with counsel, especially with regard to the most serious incidents.)

IX: ACCREDITING ASSOCIATIONS

*Hold yourself responsible for a higher standard
than anybody else expects of you.*

Henry Ward Beecher

The Critical Importance of Accrediting Associations

Associations accrediting zoological organizations serve as a first level of overlay above regulatory compliance. They provide a tremendous force for quality control and ongoing improvement via accreditation and periodic re-accreditation, aspirational statements, professional standards and guidelines, review of problematic situations, and sharing of expertise and knowledge about subjects such as animal welfare. This overlay is critically important and any zoological organization committed to EXCELLENCE BEYOND COMPLIANCE should earn and maintain accreditation as appropriate (or hold itself to similarly high standards).

Expanding the Activities of Accrediting Associations

Associations accrediting zoological organizations should expand their important efforts to provide enhanced understanding of the AWA and inspections. Accrediting associations could better serve their members and advance animal welfare through the AWA and inspections in several ways, some of which are explored below. Awareness plus action could enhance animal welfare and possibly even save animal and human lives.

1.   *Benchmarks for improvements*

One way for accrediting associations (or others, such as TAGs) to assist zoological organizations is to establish, develop and refine benchmarks for assessing animal welfare and measuring and validating improvements. Such clear, substantive benchmarks and measures for animal welfare greatly aid individual zoological organizations in implementing and validating enhancements as well as in conducting or facilitating research at their own facilities.

2.   *Cultivating researchers / research institutions to assist zoological organizations*

Accrediting associations might also help identify, develop and support a pool of researchers/research institutions to assist in important, non-invasive animal welfare-related research. Accrediting associations could, in consultation with the agency, help zoological organizations determine the appropriate role, if any, for IACUC oversight, especially with respect to non-invasive research. This would make it considerably easier for accredited zoological organizations to conduct and/or participate in important research projects. This would in turn enhance potential collaborative research involving accrediting associations and zoological organizations.[66]

3.   *Establishing a confidential, moderated distribution list mechanism*

As part of an expansion of existing activities, accrediting associations should establish a moderated, confidential distribution list for AWA compliance and related matters. An internal list or forum (electronic or otherwise) would be useful for sharing and discussing information on the AWA and inspections, and would supplement many other existing specialized lists and forums. Through a moderator (to assure anonymity, if appropriate, perhaps because of pending matters), zoological organizations could share challenges, concerns, experiences and observations arising under

---

[66] See note 13, for a classic example of such collaborative research involving a recent multi-institution elephant welfare study.

the AWA, AWA regulations and the inspection process. This could very well make zoological organization leadership and staff, as well as accrediting associations, better aware of challenges or concerns potentially relating to the animals in their care. Such a list or forum would heighten awareness about AWA concerns and issues, identify and prevent or research potential problems sooner, and disseminate ideas on improvements and responses.

4.   *Seeking advisory opinions and clarifications*

Accrediting associations should consider making greater use of seeking advisory opinions and regulatory clarifications based on unfolding events and emerging regulatory trends. Accrediting associations already do much to serve their zoological organizations with respect to functioning as a bridge and information conduit with the agency. These efforts could perhaps be complemented and expanded through earlier and even more proactive requests for clarification and guidance, including greater engagement with the Center for Animal Welfare.

5.   *Advanced AWA and inspection training*

Accrediting associations should provide the zoological community with advanced AWA and inspection training. One possibility, for example, is that the list or forum discussed above could also be combined with advanced zoological community training. The list or forum postings could also be analyzed for subjects warranting greater examination and specialized training. This would provide yet another means for reinforcing continuous improvements through constructive use of AWA processes.

6.   *Educational and mentoring programs to foster*
       improvements between accreditation inspections

The tremendous efforts zoological organizations invest in becoming accredited and in maintaining accreditation help those organizations examine and improve themselves, both from within and by virtue of the external accreditation reviews. However, in the five years *between* accreditation reviews there is not always the same impetus for prompting organizational enhancements. To make the most of the accreditation process and the expertise of accrediting associations, formal educational and mentoring programs should be administered, especially to help those organizations attaining accreditation, but also to provide support for ongoing organizational improvements in between accreditation reviews. This would help organizations become noticeably better by the time they are re-accredited, thus further underscoring the important role of accrediting associations.

7.   *Interim review between accreditation inspections*

Accrediting associations should consider developing the means for interim zoological organization review between accreditation inspections. This could take place in the absence of a crisis or problematic situation requiring review and could be funded by either the member zoological organization or perhaps via a third-party mechanism. Such interim review would provide for another level of advancement, aiding in self-assessment and continuous improvement. For example, during the accreditation process some areas in need of improvement may be identified. In such a case, the zoological organization could submit plans to address those items and then report on progress at different intervals between accreditation reviews. This would help organizations be significantly better each time they are re-accredited. It is often more cost effective to provide mentoring and to improve existing conditions before problems arise. In part, a well-executed   EXCELLENCE   BEYOND   COMPLIANCE program helps to fill this gap.

8.   *Leadership development*

Accrediting associations (and zoological organizations) should have explicit leadership development programs focused around AWA compliance and animal welfare. Accrediting association and zoological organization leadership can always be improved. Future leadership should constantly be developed. This important driver of organizational excellence should not be left to chance or ad hoc, one-off events.

9. *Additional staff and committees*

Accrediting and other professional associations should have their own Animal Welfare Officers and Committees to assist and serve zoological organizations and their professional members. The creation of such a position and group within an association sends a powerful message as to the importance of animal welfare while better equipping the association and its individual, professional and organizational members to promote excellence in animal welfare.

10. *Animal welfare programs*

Accrediting and other professional associations should conduct regular, clearly identified animal welfare programs and incorporate them into annual conferences and meetings to assist and serve zoological organizations and their individual and professional members. Accrediting and other professional associations already conduct worthwhile animal welfare programs but only sometimes are they expressly identified as such. Doing more and noting that existing programs are actually geared towards enhancing animal welfare will raise the zoological community's commitment and consciousness regarding animal welfare.

11. *Recognizing excellence*

Accrediting and other professional associations should recognize and encourage zoological organizations, their individual and professional members, APHIS Animal Care and others for contributions towards enhancing animal welfare and promoting organizational excellence. Such recognition could include, as appropriate, creating animal welfare-related awards, grants and scholarships. Accrediting and other professional associations can lead the way in positively reinforcing enhanced animal welfare and all manner of good activities in furtherance thereof.

12.   *Assisting in implementing EXCELLENCE BEYOND COMPLIANCE for zoological organizations*

Accrediting associations should consider aiding in the further development and zoological community-wide implementation of EXCELLENCE BEYOND COMPLIANCE. Making EXCELLENCE BEYOND COMPLIANCE a standard practice—perhaps even a formal program—in the zoological community would enhance animal welfare as well as AWA compliance. This would clearly reinforce the missions of accrediting associations.

13.   *EXCELLENCE BEYOND COMPLIANCE for accrediting associations*

Accrediting associations should consider incorporating EXCELLENCE BEYOND COMPLIANCE into the standards and guidelines driving their own requirements. This is the strongest measure accrediting associations could take on their own should they recommend or even require member zoological organizations to adopt and employ EXCELLENCE BEYOND COMPLIANCE. It would certainly further differentiate the membership in a positive manner that emphasizes excellence in animal welfare.

X: AGENCY MEASURES

*From a business standpoint, we need to identify
more non-regulatory solutions. Those who have heard me
speak before know this is a critical area of focus for APHIS. It is
extraordinarily difficult to gain approval for new regulations
today, and this is not likely to change anytime soon. While APHIS
will continue to have a regulatory role, it won't be the only—or in
some cases even the primary—way we contribute to animal and
plant health and animal welfare. And the reality is these
new approaches are likely to allow greater flexibility
for both APHIS and industry.*

Kevin Shea
*APHIS Administrator
July 2, 2013, Letter to Stakeholders*

There are many measures, most of which are "non-regulatory,"
which APHIS Animal Care and the Center for Animal Welfare
could consider implementing to further promote AWA compliance
and animal welfare.

1.   Pre-licensing and pre-registration training

The agency should institute pre-licensing and
pre-registration training for entities and individuals seeking
authorization to operate under the AWA. The AWA regulations
provide that full compliance with the AWA be demonstrated prior
to licensing under the AWA. Compliance is determined during the
pre-licensing inspection process. In addition to the pre-licensing
inspection, the agency should recommend and perhaps eventually
require (through a rulemaking) successful completion of

agency-approved, Center for Animal Welfare or third-party training relevant to the nature of the regulated entity's operations, especially the species of animals in their care. Rulemaking is not necessary to get started but could be in the form of the types of enhancements to the licensing process involved in the "kitchen sink" docket.[67] In the meantime, the Center for Animal Welfare should provide, and the agency should recommend, voluntary training for regulated entities.[68] The agency could also extend voluntary refresher and additional training to all regulated entities, especially in advance of license renewals.

2.   *Encouraging self-certified compliance reporting*

The agency should encourage and accept self-certified compliance reporting documenting post-inspection improvements. This will not obviate the need for reinspection where warranted under agency guidelines, but it provides an additional incentive to quickly remedy and report on corrective measures and other enhancements. It also makes agency records more accurate and up-to-date pending reinspection. More importantly, it may further speed improvements, including enhancements to animal welfare.

The agency's own Application for License Renewal (Form 7003) already provides for general self-certified compliance reporting.[69] The model EXCELLENCE BEYOND COMPLIANCE self-certified compliance reporting language included in Chapter VI: *After an Inspection* above is based on certification language contained in existing agency forms,[70] and simply goes further in recommending reporting on the corrective measures taken to remedy specifically-identified noncompliant items.

---

[67] 69 Fed. Reg. 42089 (July 14, 2004), available at:
http://www.gpo.gov/fdsys/pkg/FR-2004-07-14/pdf/04-15878.pdf
That rulemaking clarified and expanded agency authority to review certain considerations and use additional information to evaluate and perhaps deny license applications in appropriate situations.
[68] For an example of such training, see The Center for Food Security & Public Health, Introductory Course for Commercial Dog Breeders, Part 3: Maintaining Your License, Iowa State University at 22, available at:
http://www.cfsph.iastate.edu/pdf/commercial-dog-maintaining-your-license-slides
[69] See also Chapter VI: *After an Inspection*, item 4, note 33, and *Appendix A.*
[70] See also Chapter VI: *After an Inspection*, item 4.

3.   *Designating professionals/representatives to certify compliance*

The agency could facilitate self-certified compliance reporting relating to inspection report follow up through the designation/recognition of certain zoological organization officials/professionals/representatives responsible and accountable for such reporting. There are models in the U.S. Department of Agriculture, which certifies private veterinarians to inspect animals used in food production for the important protection of public health.[71] The agency could similarly accredit or recognize appropriately qualified and trained attending veterinarians or other professionals to certify compliance reporting on behalf of zoological organizations and other regulated entities.

4.   *Amending the current license renewal form*

The agency should consider amending the current license renewal form to require a copy of the most recent inspection report and a self-certified compliance statement that any noncompliant items have been corrected. Regulated entities are already required to certify overall general compliance as part of the application and renewal process.[72] This simple amendment would make regulated entities and the agency take stock of the latest reported conditions at a facility prior to renewal. It would also encourage a regulated entity (including a zoological organization) to have its house in

---

[71] See 1) USDA, APHIS, *Animal Health / Program Overview*, available at: http://www.aphis.usda.gov/wps/portal/aphis/ourfocus/animalhealth/sa_program_ overview/!ut/p/a1/rZFdb4IwFIZ_ixe7JC0F-bjET1CZy5xTuGlKBekCLZbq5n79 qtvNkulcst6d5jknb54XpGANUk4ObEsUE5xUpzl18GQeIrMHUTRe-EMY3T-PYm_mWvPQ1kCigf44CG13BiG0PQSjQS8cuH4MYeTctg8vvAD-tr8CKUgp V40qQUKakrWYCq5yrnDFMknk8Q62BIu9xIWg-_Y8Ec5qUuEyJ5Uqzz-NFFtJaiwOuTyw_PV0taFsAxILWaa5cR0jM2lh2MhxDD_zoWFZNKPE71KTk s8U34KOhz0ddDR7cKcTBKfdL-CaqDNwxUSiVbkXXfg2WPwx9eSGcpCM-_FWnyWqNBgvBFj_pEuT7GW3SwNdxkn_mwLrf2yjqZfL2rOcx_D9qahXXht 0Oh-KUuCD/?1dmy&urile=wcm%3apath%3a%2FAPHIS_Content_Library %2FSA_Our_Focus%2FSA_Animal_Health%2FSA_Program_Overview%2F

[72] See also Chapter VI: *After an Inspection*, items 4 and 7, pertaining to language adapted from APHIS Forms 7003-A (Application for New License) and 7003 (Application for License Renewal) (note 33, *Appendix A*) based upon the existing regulatory authority in 9 C.F.R. § 2.2(a) and (b).

order when renewing its license.[73] In this way the renewal process could provide a further impetus for corrective measures and other enhancements.

5.   *Providing additional species-specific information*

Agency guidance should provide more species-specific information. The *Animal Welfare Inspection Guide* is a valuable resource. There is much helpful information in this document, including, for instance, guidance on specific types of inspections and certain regulations, as well as Body Condition Assessment Charts for a number of species.[74]

One significant omission from the *Animal Welfare Inspection Guide* is the more detailed information on the substantive species-specific regulations (e.g., general facilities, primary enclosure, husbandry, transportation, records and personnel) contained in the *Animal Care Resource Guide Exhibitor Inspection Guide*, dated November 2004. To the extent possible, the agency should consider reissuing updated versions of those helpful sections. They relate to items necessary and relevant to most inspections and are especially informative for enlightened regulated entities and other stakeholders interested in better understanding the requirements of the AWA regulations.

6.   *Informal informational bulletins or "Tech Notes"*

The agency should make greater use of informal informational bulletins or "Tech Notes" to speed animal welfare enhancements. This could get advisories or generally applicable information out more quickly and in a manner which could readily enhance animal welfare. One example relates to sharing emergency information and interpretations regarding big cat containment.[75] Another involves safely housing giraffes in cold

---

[73] See Chapter VI: *After an Inspection*, item 7.
[74] See *Animal Welfare Inspection Guide* at Chapter 4 discussing different types of inspections. See also B-1 (Appendix B: Direct Noncompliance Item (NCI) Guidance); and D-1 (Appendix D: Body Condition Charts). Also see Chapter III: *Before an Inspection*, item 2.
[75] See note 19.

weather.[76] Such communications might not only enhance animal welfare but could also save animal and even human lives.

7. Highlighting better or best practices

Agency activities and guidance should do more to highlight examples of better or best practices. The AWA may be a "minimum requirements" statute, but the agency can still employ its expertise and "bully pulpit" to highlight better or best practices as a means of encouraging or reinforcing same. One very minor and simple example is found in the *Animal Welfare Inspection Guide* under "General Inspection Procedures, Inspector Safety and Etiquette" at 3-10, where it is noted, "Many licensees will have a protocol and an obvious painted 'safety line' on the floor or a barrier running adjacent to the big cat enclosures." This sort of information would be especially helpful with respect to the numerous performance-based regulations. If deemed more appropriate in order to maintain the integrity of the agency's regulatory oversight function, perhaps the Center for Animal Welfare or another third party collaborator could highlight and disseminate better or best practices information as the Center has done in the past at symposia and other meetings it has hosted and organized.

8. Positive reinforcement

The agency should do more to interject positive reinforcement into the inspection process. By its nature, the inspection process can be rather negative. While "No noncompliant items were identified during this inspection" is a meaningful statement, it is less than inspiring in showing the way towards enhanced animal welfare and even improving upon continuous compliance. Moreover, it does not take note of inspection findings where an inspector may encounter excellent examples of compliance and animal welfare in which the inspector could reinforce that behavior or light the path for other

---

[76] USDA, APHIS, Animal Care, Tech Note *Proper Giraffe Care in Cold Weather*, available at: http://www.aphis.usda.gov/animal_welfare/content/printable_version/tech%20note%20-%20giraffes%20in%20the%20cold.pdf

organizations. Whether it is a change in the inspection process to allow for positive comments (in addition to verbal remarks provided during an inspection or exit briefing), or periodic/regular agency, Center for Animal Welfare or third-party-collaborator recognition of advances and good practices, this could provide a great means for moving regulated entities towards excellence.

As stated above, these suggestions are made while being mindful of preserving the integrity of the agency's critical regulatory oversight function. For this reason the involvement of the Center for Animal Welfare or possibly other third-party collaborators in recognizing zoological organization "success stories" will likely prove vital.

9.   Expanding existing reporting

The agency should undertake to prepare timely annual or periodic reports on animal welfare advances (and perhaps on AWA compliance trends, containing rigorous stakeholder evaluation). These reports (like those on AWA enforcement, some of which are covered monthly and in summary statistics available online[77]) should be readily available to Congress, the public, media and all stakeholders. They should reinforce positive agency and stakeholder efforts and address those areas in need of improvement. While this is no substitute for ongoing, periodic Office of Inspector General (OIG) audits, it might help identify potential improvements (as well as concerns or problems) sooner. This could have a dramatic impact on animal welfare as well as AWA compliance. Periodic reports on recommendations for enhancing animal welfare would be an effective use of agency or perhaps Center for Animal Welfare time and resources.

10.   Retrospective review of prior Office of the Inspector General audits

The agency should consider a retrospective review of all prior Office of the Inspector General audits to identify and re-examine potential non-regulatory improvements. It might be helpful to revisit such past critiques to see if any contain relevant

---

[77] See note 26.

and timely suggestions for non-regulatory improvements. It could also provide a measure of regulatory advances over the years.

11. Amending the AWA regulations

The agency should consider amending the AWA regulations in order to more effectively promote animal welfare. The AWA regulations appear to contain at least three specific animal welfare-enhancing provisions: exercise for dogs;[78] environmental enhancement for nonhuman primates;[79] and enrichment for marine mammals.[80] Some provisions, like portions of the general handling regulations, may actually inhibit flexibility in varying environments and situations, and in the use of specific materials and training to explore and develop animal welfare enhancements.[81] Amendment of the regulations to allow for greater flexibility and to include additional animal-welfare-enhancing provisions in these areas would further advance the humane care and treatment of animals under the AWA.

12. Building consensus

The agency (and all stakeholders) should make better and ongoing use of negotiated rulemakings to build consensus in developing new regulations (and to avoid conflict and litigation)

---

[78] 9 C.F.R. § 3.8.

[79] 9 C.F.R. § 3.81(b).

[80] 9 C.F.R. § 3.109.

[81] For example, 9 C.F.R. § 2.131(b)(1) appears to prohibit any "behavioral stress," though of course some temporary stress may ultimately result in a beneficial change in conditions—such as when an animal's environment or social group is changed to improve its welfare. Nevertheless, even the introduction of minor temporary stress should be thoroughly reviewed and properly vetted in order to minimize or remove any potential concerns, as well as to reinforce the ultimate aim of enhancing animal welfare. Compare the prefatory language in the final rule on marine mammals, where the agency and the Marine Mammal Negotiated Rulemaking Advisory Committee noted: "No animal, regardless of the conditions of its housing and even in the wild, is without some degree of stress or discomfort at various times. A requirement that marine mammals be maintained completely without stress or discomfort would be unattainable." 66 Fed. Reg. 239, 245 (Jan 3., 2001), available at:
http://www.gpo.gov/fdsys/pkg/FR-2001-01-03/html/01-135.htm

when appropriate. One of the great success stories under the AWA is the Marine Mammal Negotiated Rulemaking, in which all interested stakeholders developed by consensus comprehensive revisions to most of the marine mammal regulations.[82] Although this process took a significant investment of time and resources, it produced new regulations without litigation, and it did so much more quickly and cost effectively than would have been possible through conventional rulemaking. The result was that the regulations were updated, all stakeholders became better informed, and animal welfare was enhanced. This should become the agency's model rather than a rare exception in its rulemaking practices.

The concept of consensus building should also be employed with regard to non-regulatory measures.[83] Less formal means can also be used to build consensus around shared interests among different stakeholders, such as a prior instance in which a number of stakeholders came together to push for additional funding for the agency.[84]

13.   Increasing agency funding

The agency's responsibilities under the AWA and the constant demands for increased action to better protect animals far exceed allocated resources. While Congress has increased agency funding over the years, the potential exists for a coalition of stakeholders to pursue additional funding supporting specific areas determined to be highly impactful in terms of immediate and long-term animal welfare enhancements.

---

[82] See Marine Mammal Negotiated Rulemaking Final Rule on Marine Mammals, 66 Fed. Reg. 251 (Jan. 3, 2001), available at:
http://www.gpo.gov/fdsys/pkg/FR-2001-01-03/html/01-135.htm

[83] The Marine Mammal Negotiated Rulemaking produced a comprehensive revision of the marine mammal regulations by consensus among all interested stakeholders, including nongovernmental organizations and the regulated and scientific communities. See 66 Fed. Reg. 239-01 (Jan. 3, 2001), available at: http://www.gpo.gov/fdsys/pkg/FR-2001-01-03/html/01-135.htm

[84] James F. Gesualdi, "Improve Administration of the Animal Welfare Act." *N. Y. St. B. J.*, 79(6) 20-21 (July/August 2007).

XI: OTHER STAKEHOLDERS: MEDIA, CRITICS, ANIMAL-RELATED ORGANIZATIONS AND THE PUBLIC

Have you learned lessons only of those who admired you, and were tender with you, and stood aside for you? Have you not learned great lessons from those who braced themselves against you, and disputed the passage with you?

Walt Whitman

1.   *Words matter*

Examples of the importance of wording are found every day in inspection reports and various other communications and statements, which can be used as teaching tools for all regulated entities and other stakeholders (though as noted earlier, inspection reports are somewhat negative in nature, as the best outcome is simply "no noncompliance"). It should be borne in mind that words can undermine a situation and make it more emotionally charged. They can also accurately portray a situation so as to facilitate an appropriate, timely and positive response which can aid AWA compliance, enhance animal welfare, advance organizational excellence and facilitate productive communication and discussion with stakeholders. Thoughtful consideration of one's language can significantly increase the likelihood of engaging in constructive conversation, even when parties may have respectful differences.

2.   *The media and the AWA*

The media plays an important role in reporting on AWA compliance and animal welfare-related matters, so it is essential that it clearly understand and communicate the implementation, administration and enforcement of the AWA. Agency staff, to the extent it does not do so already, or does so simply on a case-by-case basis, should develop a brief webinar/training module or consolidated fact sheet on the AWA specifically for the media. This training or material could be presented and then archived to remain accessible in order to continue furthering the media's understanding of the AWA and to make for the most accurate reporting of AWA requirements. (This might also be accomplished by assembling or compiling existing agency documents or publications into a brief primer on the AWA for the media and public, which could have its own weblink.[85]) It may also help in keeping the public better informed.

3.   *The role of critics, other animal-related organizations and stakeholders*

There are criticisms of zoological organizations, some of which include important ethical considerations worthy of further discussion, but most of which are beyond the scope of this book (even though many have contributed to and helped inspire the constructive approach of EXCELLENCE BEYOND COMPLIANCE towards improving animal well-being). The current reality is that zoological organizations exist lawfully and require regulation. The AWA responds to this need, and EXCELLENCE BEYOND COMPLIANCE is designed to support and enhance both AWA regulations and animal welfare *today* so as to make an immediate and ongoing difference in the lives of

---

[85] See, e.g., 1) AWA Factsheet, *Licensing and Registration Under the Animal Welfare Act: Guidelines for Dealers, Exhibitors, Transporters, and Researchers*, (issued April 1992; revised April 2004; reformatted for web August 2005 (no loss of information)), available at:
http://www.aphis.usda.gov/animal_welfare/downloads/aw/awlicreg.pdf and 2) APHIS, Animal Care, Factsheet, *Compliance Inspections* (February 2012), available at: http://www.aphis.usda.gov/publications/animal_welfare/content/printable_version/fs_compliance_inspection.pdf. See also note 9, *Appendix B.*

animals. Consequently, critics, other animal-related organizations and stakeholders should support the constructive EXCELLENCE BEYOND COMPLIANCE approach as a means of fostering animal welfare enhancements and continuous improvement above and beyond the AWA's minimum standards (and even accreditation standards). When properly administered, EXCELLENCE BEYOND COMPLIANCE will enhance animal lives.

4.   *Learning from critics, other animal-related organizations and stakeholders*

Zoological organizations should learn from critics, other animal-related organizations and stakeholders, in appropriate situations, in order to advance animal welfare. Zoological organizations operate in a complex environment within which they are one of various types of stakeholder organizations. Although they serve other stakeholders like the public, the media, and sometimes various government agencies and other animal-related organizations, they also have their critics. Some criticisms may be counterproductive; others can be constructive (even if they do not appear to be "helpful"). The best zoological organizations committed to EXCELLENCE BEYOND COMPLIANCE will work hard to find ways to learn from criticism. In such a constructive spirit, criticism is a means for accelerating organizational advancement and excellence. In many cases, the more constructive the criticism the more likely the critic may help foster and positively reinforce AWA compliance, animal welfare, and EXCELLENCE BEYOND COMPLIANCE.

Zoological organizations need not always acknowledge or directly engage critics to learn and grow from any external challenge. Likewise, more constructively-framed criticisms, as well as acknowledgements of good work and progress, would further reinforce zoological advances, all in the name of enhancing animal welfare.

5.   *Reframing the conversation about animal welfare*

The potential benefits of an ongoing dialogue between all stakeholders involved in AWA and animal welfare-related activities cannot be overstated. The EXCELLENCE BEYOND COMPLIANCE approach can serve as a framework for carrying on such conversations and for building consensus between APHIS, zoological organizations, accrediting associations, critics, other animal-related organizations and stakeholders. The constructive approach to AWA compliance and animal welfare put forth by EXCELLENCE BEYOND COMPLIANCE can also inform public discourse on the subject. The ultimate goal of these ongoing conversations, and of EXCELLENCE BEYOND COMPLIANCE as a whole, is to bring more people and resources together for the welfare of animals.

XII: THE WAY FORWARD

*Every day do something that will inch you
closer to a better tomorrow.*

Doug Firebaugh

AWA Compliance and EXCELLENCE BEYOND COMPLIANCE start with the animals and are intended to enhance animal welfare, which should be the core focus of every zoological organization. EXCELLENCE BEYOND COMPLIANCE requires ongoing commitment and ensures sustainable and lasting impact. It is designed to work synergistically with the objective of AWA compliance and to bring people together through their common love of animals and commitment to animal welfare.

There is a simple but powerful tale that begins with a man walking along a beach at low tide.[86] He encounters an individual— sometimes it's a boy or an old man, sometimes a young girl—who is picking up stranded starfish and throwing them back into the ocean. The "star-thrower" is asked why he bothers; after all, there are so many stranded starfish he could spend a year hurling them back into the ocean without making a difference. The star-thrower listens to the question as he tosses another starfish back into the water, then replies: "It makes a difference to that one."

This is what EXCELLENCE BEYOND COMPLIANCE is all about: making an even greater positive difference in the lives of animals. Though it should be initiated and reinforced by the zoological organization—and is designed to help even the most

---

[86] The original of the story, which has been adapted over the years, can be found in the science writer Loren Eiseley's essay, "The Star Thrower," originally published in *The Unexpected Universe* in 1969 (New York: Harcourt).

outstanding of these get better—EXCELLENCE BEYOND COMPLIANCE ultimately operates at the level of the individual. It is fueled by the passion that all of us have for animals, whether we are specifically their caregivers or are simply aware of them as fellow beings with whom we share the planet.

EXCELLENCE BEYOND COMPLIANCE was created to help transform the universal compassion people feel for animals into a commitment to constructive and collaborative action for their benefit on a daily basis. In the end, everyone can make a difference by giving of themselves in the service of animals.

Good intentions may be an appropriate starting point for achievement, but they will go nowhere unless you follow through with action.

Napoleon Hill

Start where you are. Use what you have. Do what you can.

Arthur Ashe

It does not matter how slowly you go up, so long as you don't stop.

Confucius

*INDEX OF APPENDICES**

Appendix A: License Application and Renewal Forms

- APHIS Form 7003A (Application for New License)
- APHIS Form 7003 (Application for License Renewal)

Appendix B: Inspection Report Notice

- USDA Inspection Report Notice

Appendix C: Inspection Report Appeals

- *Animal Welfare Inspection Guide* (2013), General Inspection Procedures, Completing the Inspection Report, Inspection Appeals Process
- APHIS, Animal Care, Factsheet, *Appeals Process* (July 2014)

Appendix D: Contingency Plans

- USDA, APHIS, Animal Care Tech Note, *Considerations When Making a Contingency Plan* (December 2012)
- APHIS, Animal Care, Factsheet *Questions and Answers: Final Rule on Contingency Plans for Regulated Entities* (January 2013)

Appendix E: Serious Incidents

- APHIS, Animal Care, Stakeholders Announcement, *Inspection Procedures in Response to an Incident or Adverse Event in Regulated Facilities* (May 11, 2012)
- APHIS, Animal Care, Factsheet, *Questions and Answers: Inspection Procedures in Response to an Incident or Adverse Event* (May 2012)

Appendix F: Enforcement Information

- Investigative and Enforcement Services Frequently Asked Questions (Last Modified April 22, 2014)

- Open Letter to Stakeholders on Investigation and Enforcement Process Streamlining (January 11, 2012)
- APHIS, Investigative and Enforcement Services, Factsheet, *Questions and Answers: APHIS Enforcement Process Streamlining* (January 2012)

Note: For easy access to the full-size, original online versions of all documents reproduced in the appendices, particularly those few that have not translated well to hardcopy, please see links on the following pages.

---

* *The United States Department of Agriculture Animal and Plant Health Inspection Service authorizes the reproduction and use of materials that are publicly available on its website. It further authorizes the use of links for information available on its website.*

Appendix A: License Application and Renewal Forms

➢ APHIS Form 7003A (Application for New License)

Available at:
http://www.aphis.usda.gov/animal_welfare/downloads/Animal%20Care%20Inspection%20Guide.pdf (A-11 at 313)

➢ APHIS Form 7003 (Application for License Renewal)

Available at:
http://www.aphis.usda.gov/animal_welfare/downloads/Animal%20Care%20Inspection%20Guide.pdf (A-13 at 315)

APHIS Form 7003A–Application for New License

According to the Paperwork Reduction Act of 1995, an agency may not conduct or sponsor, and a person is not required to respond to, a collection of information unless it displays a valid OMB control number. The valid OMB control number for this information collection is 0579-0036. The time required to complete this information collection is estimated to average .25 hours per response, including the time for reviewing instructions, searching existing data sources, gathering and maintaining the data needed, and completing and reviewing the collection of information.

OMB APPROVED 0579-0036

No license may be issued unless a completed application has been received (7 U.S.C. 2132-2143), and the applicant is in compliance with the standards and regulations Section 2133.

**UNITED STATES DEPARTMENT OF AGRICULTURE
ANIMAL AND PLANT HEALTH INSPECTION SERVICE**

APPLICATION FOR LICENSE
(TYPE OR PRINT)

NEW LICENSE

DO NOT USE THIS SPACE - OFFICIAL USE ONLY

SEND THE COMPLETED FORM TO:

LICENSE/CUSTOMER NUMBER	EXPIRATION DATE	AMOUNT	DATE RECEIVED

1. NAME OF APPLICANT AND MAILING ADDRESS: *(See Instructions)*

COUNTY: TELEPHONE NUMBER:

2. ALL BUSINESS NAMES AND LOCATION ADDRESSES HOUSING ANIMALS: INCLUDE DIRECTIONS TO EACH LOCATION *(P.O. Box not acceptable)*
☐ Use additional sheet, if necessary

COUNTY: TELEPHONE NUMBER:

3. IF THE APPLICANT IS A CORPORATION, PARTNERSHIP OR OTHER BUSINESS ENTITY, LIST THE ENTITY'S PARTNERS OR OFFICERS AND AGENT FOR SERVICE OF PROCESS.

NAME	TITLE

4. (A) PREVIOUS USDA LICENSE NUMBER: (if any)

(B) ACTIVE USDA LICENSE NUMBER IN WHICH YOU HAVE AN INTEREST:

5. TYPE OF LICENSE:
☐ Class A – Breeder   ☐ Class B – Dealer   ☐ Class C – Exhibitor

6. LIST YOUR 12 MONTH BUSINESS YEAR: *(Calendar or Fiscal)*

FROM			TO		
MO	DAY	YEAR	MO	DAY	YEAR

7. TYPE OF ORGANIZATION:
☐ Individual   ☐ Corporation   ☐ Partnership
☐ Other

8. DEALERS ONLY - CLASS A OR CLASS B LICENSES MUST COMPLETE THIS BLOCK. *(Class C Licenses go to block 9)*

CLASS A (BREEDER) – LINE "D" = ½ OF LINE "C"
CLASS B (DEALER) – LINE "D" = LINE C LESS THE PURCHASE COST OF THE ANIMALS SOLD. *(9 CFR Sections 2.6 and 2.7)*

9. EXHIBITORS ONLY - LIST THE LARGEST NUMBER OF ANIMALS THAT YOU HAVE HELD, OWNED, LEASED, OR EXHIBITED AT ANY ONE TIME DURING THE PREVIOUS BUSINESS YEAR. *(9 CFR Sections 2.6 and 2.7)*

A. ESTIMATE TOTAL NUMBER OF ANIMALS TO BE PURCHASED IN THE NEXT BUSINESS YEAR	DOGS	NONHUMAN PRIMATES	RODENTS *(Do not include lab rats or mice)*
	CATS	MARINE MAMMALS	WILD/EXOTIC HOOFSTOCK
B. ESTIMATE TOTAL NUMBER OF ANIMALS TO BE SOLD IN THE NEXT BUSINESS YEAR	GUINEA PIGS	FARM ANIMALS	BEARS
C. ESTIMATE GROSS DOLLAR AMOUNT DERIVED FROM REGULATED ACTIVITIES *(SALES, COMMISSIONS, ETC.)* $	HAMSTERS	WILD/EXOTIC CANINES	WILD/EXOTIC MAMMALS *(Not listed elsewhere)*
D. ESTIMATE DOLLAR AMOUNT ON WHICH FEE IS BASED $	RABBITS	WILD/EXOTIC FELINES	TOTAL *(All animals listed in Block 9)*

CERTIFICATION

I hereby make application for a license under the Animal Welfare Act 7 U.S.C. 2131 et seq. I certify that the information provided herein is true and correct to the best of my knowledge. I hereby acknowledge receipt of and agree to comply with all the regulations and standards in 9 CFR, Subpart A, Parts 1, 2, and 3. I certify that the applicant is 18 years of age or older.

10. SIGNATURE:	11. PRINT NAME AND TITLE:	12. DATE:

APHIS FORM 7003A
AUG 2011   *(Previous editions are obsolete)*

Figure A-7 APHIS Form 7003A–Application for New License

APHIS Form 7003–Application for License Renewal

Figure A-8 APHIS Form 7003–Application for License Renewal

Appendix B: Inspection Report Notice

➢ • USDA Inspection Report Notice

Available at:
http://www.aphis.usda.gov/animal_welfare/downloads/IR_
Explanation.pdf

NOTICE

The Animal Welfare Act (AWA) requires that humane care and treatment be provided for certain warm-blooded animals that are exhibited to the public, bred for commercial sale, used in biomedical research or transported commercially. Entities licensed or registered with USDA must provide their animals with adequate care and treatment in the areas of housing, handling, sanitation, nutrition, water, veterinary care and protection from extreme weather and temperatures. The AWA excludes animals raised for food or fiber.

To ensure that AWA standards are being met, inspectors from USDA's Animal and Plant Health Inspection Service (APHIS) conduct routine, comprehensive inspections of licensed and registered facilities and animals – assessing all areas of care and treatment covered by the AWA. These inspections are unannounced, thereby giving inspectors a genuine sense of how licensees and registrants are caring for their animals. The noncompliant items observed by the inspector are documented on an inspection report, and these reports portray the conditions that inspectors found at the time of the inspection. The inspection reports are posted online as public information on APHIS' website.

APHIS' goal is for all AWA-regulated facilities to be in full compliance every day. Inspectors are trained to identify and document all non-compliant items on the inspection reports. In some cases, a licensee or registrant will correct a non-compliant item at the time of inspection and the inspector can document that the item was corrected on the report. Otherwise, the inspector will set a deadline for the non-compliant item to be corrected. At some point after the deadline, a re-inspection will take place. The timing of the re-inspection depends on a number of risk factors, including the nature of the non-compliant item and the overall compliance history of the facility. Although the inspector may follow up to confirm corrective action was taken, corrected non-compliant items will not show up on subsequent inspection reports.

In situations where identified non-compliant items are not corrected within the specified timeframe, APHIS takes appropriate enforcement action. Violations of the AWA can lead to penalties, including official warnings, fines and license suspensions/revocations. Completed APHIS enforcement actions are posted as monthly press releases; these releases can be found at http://www.aphis.usda.gov/animal_welfare/index.shtml.

*Please note that the link to monthly press releases for completed APHIS enforcement actions is now:
http://www.aphis.usda.gov/wps/portal/aphis/newsroom/news.

Appendix C: Inspection Report Appeals

➢ *Animal Welfare Inspection Guide* (2013), General Inspection Procedures, Completing the Inspection Report, Inspection Appeals Process

Available at:
http://www.aphis.usda.gov/animal_welfare/downloads/Animal%20Care%20Inspection%20Guide.pdf (3-27 to 3-29 at 61 – 63)

➢ APHIS, Animal Care, Factsheet, *Appeals Process* (July 2014)

Available at:
http://www.aphis.usda.gov/publications/animal_welfare/2014/appeals_process.pdf

If, at the time of the inspection, a licensee/registrant anticipates that an extension will be needed:

1. Explain to him/her how to request an extension.

2. Document on the Inspection Report that the procedure for requesting an extension was explained to the licensee.

NOTICE

Extensions are for special circumstances. Do **not** suggest an extension to the licensee for correction of routine noncompliant items.

An extension request, whether anticipated or unexpected, **must** be:

1. In writing

2. Appropriate, i.e., **only** for indirect NCI related to facility maintenance

3. Specific as to the reason/justification for the request

> **EXAMPLE**   ◆ Unexpected delays during the correction process, such as budget or severe weather delays
> ◆ Unforeseen special circumstances that prevent completion, such as death or serious illness in the family

4. Sent to the appropriate Animal Care (AC) Regional Office

5. Received by the AC Regional Office **prior** to the original correction date

The Regional Office will notify the licensee/registrant, in writing, whether or **not** the extension was granted.

Inspection Appeals Process

If the licensee/registrant has a concern about any findings on the Inspection Report, use the inspection appeals process to resolve the dispute.

Prior to Finalizing the Inspection Report

If a licensee/registrant/facility representative has questions or concerns about a noncompliant item(s) cited on the Inspection Report, you, the inspector, should explain why the noncompliance was cited and give the facility representative the opportunity to provide additional information pertinent to the findings at the exit briefing. If the concern is resolved, amend the citation. If the concern **cannot** be resolved:

1. Inform the licensee/registrant/facility representative of the next step in the appeals process.

2. Give the licensee/registrant/facility representative a copy of the appeals process fact sheet.

If there was an unresolved disputed noncompliance:

◆ Finalize the inspection report

◆ Inform your SACS that there may be an appeal of a noncompliance item(s) cited on the inspection report

After Finalizing the Inspection Report

If a licensee/registrant/facility representative has questions or concerns about a noncompliant item(s) cited on the Inspection Report, meet with the licensee/registrant/facility representative, if requested, to discuss the noncompliance.

If you and the licensee/registrant/facility representative resolve the disagreement on the noncompliance, generate an amended Inspection Report and inform your SACS of the resolution. Give or send (by certified, return receipt mail) a copy of the Inspection Report to the licensee/registrant. Send a copy of the amended Inspection Report to the Regional Office.

If the dispute **cannot** be resolved, inform the licensee/registrant/facility representative of the next step in the appeals process. Give the licensee/registrant/facility representative a copy of the appeals process fact sheet. Inform your SACS that there may be an appeal of a noncompliance item(s) cited on the Inspection Report.

If the licensee/registrant's appeal of a noncompliance is determined to be valid, i.e., a citation is to be modified or deleted, a new, amended Inspection Report will be generated in ACIS by the Regional Office with SACS concurrence.

If the licensee/registrant's appeal of noncompliance is determined to be invalid, the SACS will write a letter to the licensee/registrant/facility representative informing him/her of the decision. The inspector will receive a copy of the letter.

NOTICE

Inspection appeals should **not** delay reinspection of direct noncompliances or interfere with efforts to ensure that the immediate welfare needs of the animals are met.

Amended Inspection Report

The amended inspection report should:

1. Be dated the date that the actual inspection was conducted in "Inspection Date" block

2. Be dated the date that the amended inspection report was signed or sent to the licensee/registrant in the "Signature Block."

3. Cite any noncompliances that were modified on appeal.

4. Cite the noncompliances that were **not** appealed or overturned on appeal.

NOTICE

The citation on the amended Inspection Report **must** be identical to the citation on the unmodified original Inspection Report.

5. Contain the statement: "This is an amended report of inspection report." (*ACIS inspection "d" code of original inspection report located at the top of the inspection report*).

If the inspector generates the amended inspection report, send a copy of the inspection report to the:

◆ Licensee/registrant by certified, return receipt mail

◆ SACS or Regional Office.

If the SACS generates the amended inspection report, send a copy of the Inspection Report to the:

◆ Inspector

◆ Licensee/registrant by certified, return receipt mail

◆ Regional Office

Mistakes on the Inspection Report

Read the inspection report carefully before printing and finalizing to ensure that all information and spelling are correct.

Prior to Printing the Final Inspection Report

To make the inspection report as accurate as possible, ensure that:

1. You are entering the inspection:

    A. Under the correct licensee/registrant

    B. Under the correct certificate number

    C. In the correct site

2. All information is entered into the database correctly, such as:

    A. Inspection type

    B. Name and title of person signing the inspection report

3. All information in the narrative is correct, such as:

    A. Citation Section and subsections

    B. Regulation or standard correctly paraphrased, if applicable

    C. Buildings/locations inspected, if appropriate

    D. Location of inspection of a TRA site

Animal Care

USDA United States
Department of
Agriculture

Animal and Plant Health Inspection Service
APHIS 41-05-015

www.aphis.usda.gov/animal_welfare   July 2014   Factsheet

Appeals Process

Animal Care, a part of the U.S. Department of Agriculture (USDA), enforces the Animal Welfare Act primarily through inspections of regulated facilities. However, Animal Care understands that sometimes there may be concerns about what its inspectors cite on inspection reports. It is in the best interest of the involved facility, Animal Care, and, above all, the welfare of the animals to resolve any concerns over inspection findings quickly and cooperatively.

■ Goals

With this in mind, Animal Care has established a new process for licensees and registrants regulated under the Animal Welfare Act who wish to appeal something that has been cited on their USDA inspection report. The goal for this new process is threefold: to bring about quicker appeals resolutions; to maintain consistency in the appeals process; and to ensure that subject matter experts are involved in reviewing each appeal.

■ Revised Appeals Process

The revised appeals process is as follows:

1) During an inspection, if a USDA inspector observes that a facility is not in full compliance with Animal Welfare Act requirements, the inspector will cite the noncompliant item(s) on the inspection report and explain the citation(s) to the facility operator. If the facility operator has questions or concerns about the inspector's findings, the facility operator should bring the issue up with the inspector during the course of the inspection and/or during the exit briefing. If the matter is resolved at that time, the inspector will modify the citation, remove it altogether, or leave it as originally written.

2) If the facility operator and the inspector are unable to resolve the matter, or if the facility later decides to question the report, the facility operator should send a detailed, written appeal to the regional director in the appropriate Animal Care regional office. Animal Care must receive this appeal within 21 days of the facility receiving the finalized inspection report. If the appeal is received after the 21-day period, it will be rejected.

3) If no appeal is filed, Animal Care will make inspection reports publicly available on its Web site 21 days from the date they are finalized. If the inspection report is appealed, the inspection report will not be publicly available until a final decision on the appeal is made.

4) An Animal Care appeals team will review each appeal. Each team consists of a director from one region and an assistant director from the other region—plus an Animal Care field or staff veterinarian who serves as a subject matter expert, based on the specifics of the appeal. Within 3 weeks of receiving an appeal, the assigned team will either make a final decision or request more information. All decisions made by the appeals teams are final and represent USDA's final determination of compliance. If the inspection report is amended, only the final report will be made available online.

■ Commitment to Objectivity and Thoroughness

Animal Care realizes that disagreements are a natural part of regulatory oversight, and inspectors understand that regulated facilities have the right to appeal inspection findings. Animal Care is committed to ensuring that the appeals process is objective and thorough, while not resulting in reprisal against any facility. The new appeals process is a way to streamline and improve decision making so that USDA Animal Care can better serve the regulated community, the general public, and the animals.

[continued, reverse side]

Animal Care

Factsheet

United States
Department of
Agriculture

www.aphis.usda.gov/animal_welfare

■ **Additional Information**

If you would like more information about the inspection report appeals process, or if you are a licensee or registrant seeking to file an appeal, please contact the appropriate USDA Animal Care regional office based on your geographic location:

Eastern Regional Office

USDA Animal Care

920 Main Campus Drive, Suite 200

Raleigh, NC 27606-5210

Phone: (919) 855-7100

Fax: (919) 855-7125

Email: aceast@aphis.usda.gov

Western Regional Office

USDA Animal Care

2150 Centre Avenue, Building B, Mailstop #3W11

Fort Collins, CO 80526-8117

Phone: (970) 494-7478

Fax: (970) 494-7461

Email: acwest@aphis.usda.gov

*Appendix D: Contingency Plans**

➢ USDA, APHIS, Animal Care Tech Note, *Considerations When Making a Contingency Plan* (December 2012)

Available at:
http://www.aphis.usda.gov/animal_welfare/content/printabl e_version/contingency_rule_tech.pdf

This Tech Note contains the best, most concise guidance for preparing contingency plans.

➢ APHIS, Animal Care, Factsheet *Questions and Answers: Final Rule on Contingency Plans for Regulated Entities* (January 2013)

Available at:
http://www.aphis.usda.gov/animal_welfare/content/printabl e_version/contingency_rule_faq.pdf

* "Effective July 31, 2013, USDA issued a stay of the AWA Contingency Plan regulation. [78 Fed. Reg. 46255 (July 31, 2013) (temporary stay of the Contingency Plan regulation)] This means that, until further notice, dealers, exhibitors, intermediate handlers, carriers and research facilities using animals covered by the AWA do not have to comply with the contingency planning, training and other requirements of the Contingency Plan regulation."[87]

These materials still provide helpful information about the substance of contingency plans and contingency planning, and are thus highly relevant to organizations committed to EXCELLENCE BEYOND COMPLIANCE.

---

[87] See "Animal Welfare Act Contingency Plan Final Rule," 77 Fed Reg. 76823 (Dec. 31, 2012) at: http://www.aphis.usda.gov/wps/portal/aphis/ourfocus/ animalwelfare?1dmy&urile=wcm%3Apath%3A/aphis_content_library/sa_our_f ocus/sa_animal_welfare/sa_awa/ct_awa_contingency_regulation_final_rule

December 2012

Considerations When Making a Contingency Plan

Dealers, exhibitors, research facilities, intermediate handlers, carriers and other entities regulated under the Animal Welfare Act are now required to take steps to be prepared for emergencies and disasters. An emergency plan, also referred to as a "contingency plan," safeguards the animals should an emergency or disaster occur and supports the facility's response to emergencies and recovery from emergencies most likely to happen to their facility. Employees and other personnel involved in animal care or business processes should be aware of the facility's contingency plan and sufficiently trained on it.

This tech note provides general considerations a facility can take into account when designing its own contingency plan. There is *no* required format or length for a facility's contingency plan. APHIS wants these plans to be useful for the facility and beneficial for the animals during potential disaster situations. Individual facilities have the freedom to design their plans to best suit their facility, location and needs. Dealers, exhibitors and research facilities housing animals at holding facilities need to include these holding facilities in their contingency plan if the holding facility does not have its own contingency plan. APHIS inspectors are available for assistance in reviewing and developing plans, as needed.

Specific details of the Animal Welfare Act regulations regarding contingency plans can be found here:
9 CFR, Part 2, Subpart C, § 2.38(l)(1)(i-iv) and Subpart I, § 2.134(a)(1-4); Subpart H, § 2.102(a)(4) and (b)(3) 9 CFR, Part 2, Subpart C, § 2.38(i)(4).

Based on the regulations, the following five basic elements should be addressed in the plan.

1. Common emergencies likely to happen to your facility
The terms "emergency" and "disaster" are not limited to major natural disasters, such as hurricanes, and should include consideration of localized events such as a fire, severe weather or any other unexpected situation that interrupts normal animal care activities. Some possible emergencies to consider include, but are not limited to:

- structural fire
- electrical outage
- disruption in clean water or feed supply
- disruption in access to facility (e.g. road closures)
- intentional attack on the facilities/animals/personnel
- hazardous materials situation
- employee absence
- unexpected change in ownership
- faulty heating, ventilation and air conditioning (HVAC) system

- animal escape
- animal disease outbreak
- flooding
- earthquake
- landslide/mudslide/avalanche
- hurricane
- tornado
- blizzard/ice storm
- extreme heat/humidity
- wildfire

2. Specific tasks to be taken during emergencies
Depending on the circumstances and type of emergency, a facility should decide for itself whether its animals and employees should be relocated. Facilities housing animals should also have a plan for animal escapes.

Sheltering-in-place. Animals remain in primary enclosures during an emergency and employees stay on premises to provide animal care.
- husbandry and care needs for the animals (e.g. food and water)
- access to a veterinarian

Tech Note: USDA APHIS Animal Care Animal Welfare Act Contingency Plan Regulation

Sheltering-in-place (continued):
- staffing and housing options (including food and water) for the staff
- environmental conditions (e.g. temperature, ventilation, lighting)
- animal identification
- records maintenance

Evacuation. Animals are moved out of their primary enclosure to another location, either on the grounds of the facility or to a remote location.
- transportation vehicle(s) and equipment/caging
- alternate location(s) for housing animals: These locations should be included on the facility's contingency plan.
- husbandry and care needs for the animals during transport and once animals are relocated
- environmental conditions on transportation vehicle and at alternate location(s)
- staffing during transport and at the alternative location
- animal identification
- records transfer

Escaped animal(s)
- supplies needed (e.g. communication equipment, gloves, nets, drugs, darting equipment)
- secondary barriers secured
- employee/public safety procedures
- notification of emergency response/security/law enforcement personnel
- recovery/transport of animal(s) back to original enclosure

3. Chain-of-command for implementing the plan
Pre-assigning responsibility to personnel for the tasks identified above as part of the planning process can streamline your response during an emergency by establishing clear authority structures and lines of communication.
- Identify the person who has the authority to initiate the contingency plan.
- Identify the people (or positions) in charge of the tasks listed in the plan.
- Have an updated contact list distributed to all of the people involved in the plan.
- Identify the methods to be used to maintain communication.

4. Materials and resources required for response and recovery
Facilities have the freedom to decide which equipment and materials they will need to make possible the tasks identified in their contingency plans. Arrangements should be made for how the facility is going to obtain the equipment during an emergency if it is not on-hand, as well as determining if certification or other specialized training is required for the use of any equipment.
- Identify and list materials and resources necessary to implement the plan.
- Obtain the necessary materials or have a plan for obtaining the materials during an emergency

5. Employee training on the plan
Ensuring that employees are aware of the plan and understand their roles will result in more expedient and organized responses during an emergency. "Employees," in this sense, refers not only to paid staff but also to volunteers and others involved in animal care and/or integral to the business operation.
- On your contingency plan, document any and all training provided to your employees.
- Ensure that employees are aware of any changes to the plan or their assigned roles.

APHIS   Factsheet

Animal Care   January 2013

Questions and Answers: Final Rule on Contingency Plans for Regulated Entities

Q. What does this rule do?
A. On December 31, 2012, the U.S. Department of Agriculture's (USDA) Animal and Plant Health Inspection Service (APHIS) published a final rule requiring all dealers, exhibitors, intermediate handlers, carriers, research facilities and other entities regulated by the agency under the Animal Welfare Act (AWA) to take additional steps to be better prepared for potential disaster situations. They are required to develop a plan for how they are going to respond to and recover from emergencies most likely to happen to their facility, as well as train their employees on those plans. These emergency plans are also referred to as "contingency plans."

Q. Why is this rule necessary?
A. The goal of this rule is to increase the regulated community's awareness and understanding about their responsibilities to protect their animals in emergency situations. Developing contingency plans could potentially save the lives of their animals—and their employees—during an emergency or natural disaster. It will also allow each USDA licensee and registrant to evaluate their preparedness and to more fully understand how they can better survive a disaster or emergency situation.

Q. Why are contingency plans important?
A. The need for contingency planning was emphasized by events experienced by several coastal facilities during the 2005 hurricane season, including Hurricane Katrina, where animals escaped and damaged communication lines impaired communication between employers and employees. Lessons learned from such instances have shown that when people have a plan for an emergency, the response to that emergency can be more effective.

Q. How will the contingency planning process help me?
Taking the time to prepare a contingency plan and think through potential emergencies will help protect your animals. Following a contingency plan will also help with continuity of operations and potentially shorten the time needed to return to fully operational status following an emergency. When staff members are properly trained in what to do during emergencies or disasters, they are better able to safeguard the facility's animals—and themselves.

Q. What information is required in the contingency plans?
A. APHIS Animal Care wants these plans to be simple and useful for the regulated community. Those regulated by APHIS under the AWA have the freedom to design their plans to best suit their facility, location, and needs.

However, there are a few basic elements that need to be included:
- identify common emergencies that could occur at their particular type of facility;
- outline specific tasks that the facility staff will undertake in an emergency situation;
- establish a clear chain of command for all employees to follow; and
- identify materials and resources for use during an emergency that are available at that facility or elsewhere and affirm that all employees are trained on the contents of the plan.

Q. What training is required?
A. Each regulated entity must properly train all pertinent employees on the contingency plan. This ensures that they are aware of the plan, understand the role they play in the plan, and are ready to take action should an emergency occur. If the contingency plan is modified, the regulated entity is also required to let employees know within 30 days.

Q. Do I have to send my plan to APHIS?
A. No, you are not required to send a copy of your plan to APHIS. Facilities will keep their own plans and show them to APHIS Animal Care inspectors upon request. Our intent is not to sign off on or certify these plans, but rather to make sure that our facilities have gone through the planning process in a manner that works best for them. That being said, inspectors will work with facilities on improving plans, if they identify gaps upon review of those plans.

Q. When do I need to have my plan ready?

A. A written plan must be in place at all USDA-licensed and -registered facilities by July 29, 2013, but facilities are not required to share that plan with the inspector to review until the facility has had a chance to train all its employees on that plan. All employees must be trained on the plan by September 27, 2013. Thus, contingency plans should be available upon request by APHIS inspectors after September 27, 2013. Should facilities need review of the plan prior to training their employees, they are welcome to discuss it with their inspectors.

Q. What if we have an emergency and the plan we had in place didn't work?

A. We understand that the true impact of an emergency cannot be fully anticipated or predicted, thus certain aspects of a plan may fail. Emergency preparedness is an ever-evolving process, and lessons learned from actual experience can impact planning efforts, and we encourage incorporating those lessons learned into a revised plan. Once a plan is revised, a facility has 30 days to retrain its employees on that new plan.

Q. What resources are available to help me in the planning process?

A. APHIS is currently planning a series of three live Webinars, including question and answer sessions, to share information with the regulated community and interested stakeholders. Animal Care will also help educate the regulated community about ways it can better prepare for emergencies.

APHIS will provide guidance documents on its Web site to help regulated entities with their planning, and written materials will be available as well, along with reference materials, such as examples of contingency plans from facilities.

Q. What if I already have a contingency plan in place?

A. We understand that there are facilities that may already have a plan in place as required by their State or an accreditation process (e.g., Public Health Service assurance, Association of Zoos and Aquariums accreditation, or Association for Assessment and Accreditation of Laboratory Animal Care International certification). If these plans meet the basic requirements for contingency plans under the AWA as described in this regulation, they will not have to be changed.

Q. Will all facilities regulated by APHIS be required to have a contingency plan?

A. We are aware that there may be unique situations or circumstances where having a written contingency plan as described in the regulation may not be practical or feasible. For example, some facilities do not hold animals for a prolonged period of time. APHIS is working on guidance for such facilities, and until that guidance is released, these situations will be assessed on a case-by-case basis.

Q. Marine mammals are already required under the AWA to have plans for emergency sources for electricity and water. How does this rule apply to these types of facilities?

A. In addition to meeting requirements already described for them in the AWA, facilities housing marine mammals must also have a contingency plan in place that meets the requirements of this new rule.

USDA is an equal opportunity provider and employer.

Appendix E: Serious Incidents

➢ APHIS, Animal Care, Stakeholders Announcement, *Inspection Procedures in Response to an Incident or Adverse Event in Regulated Facilities* (May 11, 2012)

Available at:
http://www.aphis.usda.gov/publications/animal_welfare/2012/inspection_incident_response_sa.pdf

➢ APHIS, Animal Care, Factsheet, *Questions and Answers: Inspection Procedures in Response to an Incident or Adverse Event* (May 2012)

Available at:
http://www.aphis.usda.gov/publications/animal_welfare/2012/inspection_incident_response_faq.pdf

APHIS

Stakeholders Announcement

Animal Care

May 11, 2012

Inspection Procedures in Response to an Incident or Adverse Event in Regulated Facilities

With this announcement, the U.S. Department of Agriculture's (USDA) Animal and Plant Health Inspection Service (APHIS) seeks to provide clear direction to research facilities, exhibitors, dealers, carriers, and intermediate handlers on procedures for reporting incidents and adverse events and to clarify how the agency responds to such notifications in accordance with the Animal Welfare Act (AWA) and the Animal Welfare Regulations (AWR).

An incident or adverse event is an occurrence that includes but is not limited to:

- Facility disasters, such as floods or fires;
- Mishandling or escapes;
- Attacks and fighting between animals as a result of incompatibility;
- Human injury as a result of an animal attack;
- Injury or death related to cage washers, environmental enrichment devices, and squeeze or guillotine mechanisms; and
- Failures in HVAC systems, automatic feeders, or watering systems.

There is no regulatory requirement that AWA licensees or registrants report incidents or adverse events to APHIS Animal Care, with the exception of an event that results in the suspension of a protocol at a research facility (in accordance with AWR § 2.31 [d][7]). Licensees and registrants may choose to report incidents or adverse events in order to advise Animal Care of the situation, provide documentation of their corrective actions, or demonstrate their good faith intention to comply with the AWA and regulations.

Animal Care may conduct an inspection in response to a facility reporting an incident or adverse event. However, a citation will not be indicated on the inspection report if the following factors are evident:

- The licensee/registrant found the problem in a timely manner,
- The incident or adverse event was not reasonably foreseeable,
- Timely and appropriate corrective action was taken to prevent a recurrence,
- There is no ongoing pattern of violations at the facility, and
- There were no serious animal welfare impacts.

A noncompliance item (NCI) will be placed in the report if the incident had a severe impact on animal health and well-being, the problem was not identified and/or corrected in a timely manner, the incident was reasonably foreseeable, or there is an ongoing pattern of violations. If the problem is not corrected by the date assigned by the inspector, it will be listed as a Repeat NCI on the next inspection report.

Some incidents or adverse events will be followed by an announced visit from Animal Care as an effort to ensure that the facility has appropriate personnel and documentation available. These post-incident visits will not, however, take the place of Animal Care's regular, unannounced compliance inspections.

Note to Stakeholders: Stakeholders announcements and other APHIS information are available on the Internet at www.aphis.usda.gov. For additional information on this topic, contact Dave Sacks at (301) 851-4079 or email david.sacks@aphis.usda.gov.

APHIS

Factsheet

Animal Care

May 2012

Questions and Answers: Inspection Procedures in Response to an Incident or Adverse Event

Q. What is an incident or adverse event?

A. Incidents and adverse events at facilities regulated under the Animal Welfare Act (AWA) include but are not limited to: floods, fires, or other facility disasters; animal mishandling or escapes; attacks and fighting between animals as a result of incompatibility; human injury as a result of an animal attack; failures in HVAC systems, automatic feeders, or watering systems; and injury or death related to cage washers, environmental enrichment devices, and squeeze or guillotine mechanisms.

Q. Should incidents and adverse events be reported to Animal Care by the licensee/registrant?

A. There is no regulatory requirement that licensees or registrants report incidents or adverse events to Animal Care (a division of the U.S. Department of Agriculture [USDA], Animal and Plant Health Inspection Service [APHIS]), with the exception of an event that results in the suspension of a protocol at a research facility. Licensees and registrants may choose to report incidents or adverse events in order to advise Animal Care of the situation, provide documentation of their corrective actions, and demonstrate their good faith intention to comply with the AWA and regulations.

Q. Will incidents and adverse events be cited as noncompliance items (NCIs) on an Animal Care inspection report?

A. These types of events will not be cited as NCIs if (1) the licensee/registrant found the problem in a timely manner, (2) the incident or adverse event was not reasonably foreseeable, (3) the licensee/registrant took timely and appropriate corrective action to prevent a recurrence, (4) there is not an ongoing pattern of violations at the facility, and (5) there were no serious animal welfare impacts as a result of the event. However, if there were serious animal welfare impacts, the problem was not identified and/or corrected in a timely manner, the incident was reasonably foreseeable, or there is an ongoing pattern of violations, Animal Care will cite the event as an NCI.

Q. Will incidents and adverse events that are cited get a correction date?

A. An NCI that resulted in serious animal welfare impacts will be assigned a correction date. If applicable, the inspector may document on the inspection report that the NCI was corrected during the inspection. If the citation is a repeat of a previous citation, the NCI will be listed as a Repeat NCI on the report, and no correction date will be given.

Q. Will Animal Care inspections in response to incidents or adverse events be announced?

A. Routinely, Animal Care conducts unannounced inspections to determine if facilities are in compliance with the AWA regulations and standards. In an effort to ensure that a facility has appropriate personnel and documentation available, Animal Care may conduct an announced visit to evaluate an incident or adverse event. These post-incident visits do not, however, take the place of regular, unannounced compliance inspections.

Additional Information

For more information about the AWA and its regulations and standards, visit the APHIS Animal Care Web site at **www.aphis.usda.gov/animal_welfare.** You can also contact the program's headquarters office at:

Animal Care, APHIS-USDA
4700 River Road, Unit 84
Riverdale, MD 20737-1234
Phone: (301) 851-3751
Fax: (301) 734-4978
Email: ace@aphis.usda.gov

USDA is an equal opportunity provider and employer.

Appendix F: Enforcement Information

➤ Investigative and Enforcement Services Frequently Asked Questions (Last Modified September 23, 2014)

Available at:
http://www.aphis.usda.gov/wps/portal/aphis/ourfocus/busin ess-services?urile=wcm%3Apath%3A/aphis_content_ library/ sa_our_focus/sa_business_services/sa_investigative _enforcement/ct_ies_faq

➤ Open Letter to Stakeholders on Investigation and Enforcement Process Streamlining (January 11, 2012)

Available at:
http://www.aphis.usda.gov/ies/pdf/ies_stakeholders_letter.p df

➤ APHIS, Investigative and Enforcement Services, Factsheet, *Questions and Answers: APHIS Enforcement Process Streamlining* (January 2012)

Available at:
http://www.aphis.usda.gov/publications/aphis_general/201 2/IES_process.pdf

 Animal and Plant Health Inspection Service

United States Department of Agriculture

IES Frequently Asked Questions

I've been notified that I am under investigation. What does this mean.
IES investigates alleged violations of APHIS-administered laws and issues enforcement actions. If one of our Investigators notifies you that you are the subject of an investigation, IES generally has preliminary information indicating that you may have been involved in a regulatory violation involving animal or plant health. IES conducts an investigation (or, fact finding process) to determine the facts relating to the alleged violation through interviews, photographs, witness statements, etc. An Investigator will ask you to participate in this process to assist IES in gaining a full understanding of the facts and circumstances surrounding the alleged violation?

Who should I contact for information about the status of an investigation?
Because the investigative process is fluid, we typically cannot discuss the facts of an investigation while the case remains open. The Investigator who visited with you can refer you to the enforcement staff for additional information involving the investigation or tell when you when an investigation is closed, as appropriate.

What types of enforcement actions can APHIS take?
APHIS has several enforcement options, including issuing an official warning, offering a pre-litigation settlement agreement, referring the matter to the Office of the General Counsel for litigation, or referring the matter to other external authorities, such as the USDA Office of the Inspector General for criminal investigation or U.S. Department of Justice for civil or criminal action.

How does APHIS determine penalty amounts for settlements?
If APHIS determines that a civil penalty is appropriate, it calculates the penalty according to the applicable APHIS civil penalty guidelines. APHIS's animal and plant health laws include penalty provisions, which often include the minimum or maximum civil penalty amount and specific factors that the agency should consider when determining the appropriate penalty. Depending on the applicable law, these factors may (or may not) include the nature, circumstance, extent, seriousness, and gravity of the alleged violation, the degree of culpability of the person involved, the person's history of violations, the size or nature of the person's business, whether the person involved demonstrated good faith and/or cooperated with the investigation, the person's ability to pay, the effect of the penalty on the person's ability to continue business, and other appropriate factors. APHIS's civil penalty guidelines ensure that the agency takes into account the minimum and maximum penalty amount and the specific factors listed in the applicable statute. They also ensure that penalties are calculated fairly and consistently. It is APHIS's practice to periodically review its penalty guidelines to assess whether they are functional, equitable, and effective in discouraging violations of APHIS's animal and plant health laws, to incorporate new developments in the Department's Agriculture Decisions, and to be consistent with adjustments for inflation and statutory changes.

What are the general terms of pre-litigation settlements?
In general, a pre-litigation settlement agreement offers an alleged violator the opportunity to resolve alleged violations of APHIS's animal and plant health laws by paying a monetary civil penalty or agreeing to specific non-monetary terms within the specified time period. The alleged violator agrees to waive his or her right to a hearing.

For monetary settlement agreements, APHIS typically offers to settle for a civil penalty that is much lower than the maximum civil penalty authorized in the relevant statute. The alleged violator can pay the penalty by check, money order, or credit card, following the instructions provided with the settlement agreement. If someone is unable to pay the full amount by the due date provided on the settlement agreement, he or she may be eligible for a payment plan. To request a payment plan, the alleged violator should use the form enclosed with the settlement agreement to submit a written response, indicating that he or she wishes to pay the penalty and waive his or her right to a hearing.

For non-monetary settlement agreements, APHIS may offer to settle based on the alleged violator's agreement to specific terms that generally involve abstaining from APHIS-regulated activities. For example, for non-monetary settlement agreements issued under the Animal Welfare Act (AWA), an alleged violator may agree to the revocation of his or her AWA license and/or his or her agreement to sell, donate, and/or transfer ownership of his or her regulated animals.

If you receive a pre-litigation settlement agreement (either a monetary or non-monetary settlement agreement), you should review the information carefully for the specific terms.

I do not agree with the settlement terms. What are my other options?
If you do not agree with the terms of the settlement agreement, submit a request for a hearing, with your Reference Number, to our office by the due date provided on the settlement agreement, at 4700 River Rd., Unit 85, Riverdale, MD

20737, or call the enforcement staff member assigned to your case. You can find his or her name in the cover letter that accompanied the settlement agreement. You are also welcome to call our main office at (301) 851-2948.

I have questions about the enforcement action that I received. Who should I call?

If you have any questions concerning an enforcement action, you should contact the IES staff member assigned to your case. You can find his or her name in the cover letter that accompanied your official warning or settlement agreement. You are also welcome to call our main office at (301) 851-2948.

What happens if I do not respond to a settlement agreement?

If we do not receive a payment or hearing request from you by the due date provided on the settlement agreement, we will forward the matter to our Office of the General Counsel for litigation. APHIS may file an administrative complaint through the Office of the General Counsel. The Rules of Practice Applicable to Proceedings Pending Before the Secretary of Agriculture govern the proceeding.

I am a small business owner and have comments or concerns regarding APHIS's enforcement of animal and plant health laws. Who should I contact?

APHIS always welcomes comments on how it can better assist small businesses. If you have comments about APHIS's enforcement of animal and plant health laws, please contact Bernadette Juarez, the APHIS Small Business Ombudsperson, at 301-851-2948. If you would prefer to comment to someone outside APHIS, you may contact the Small Business Regulatory Enforcement Ombudsperson at http://sba.gov/ombudsman, email ombudsman@sba.gov, or toll free at 1-888-REG-FAIR. The Ombudsperson's office receives comments from small businesses and annually evaluates federal agency enforcement activities for their responsiveness to the special needs of small businesses.

Does IES have any system of quality control for its work?

IES has developed and implemented a Quality Management System (QMS) that is certified to the International Organization for Standardization (ISO) 9001:2008 internationally recognized requirements for quality management systems. IES developed its QMS to measure, analyze, and continually improve the quality of its services to better satisfy the needs of APHIS's regulatory enforcement programs. The QMS guides workflow within IES, and ensures that IES Enforcement employees are following the guidance and procedures that will allow them to review and respond to alleged violations in an equitable and consistent manner.

IES' QMS receives annual audits from the an independent audit services firm. Since 2011, IES external audits have all resulted in findings of "no nonconformities" with the ISO standard.

United States
Department of
Agriculture

Animal and Plant
Health Inspection
Service

Washington, DC
20250

JAN 1 1 2012

Open Letter to Stakeholders:

As a regulatory agency, our mission to protect plant health, animal health, and the welfare of animals is a critical one. And, we are very serious about taking enforcement action against those who jeopardize this mission by violating our regulations. In recent years, APHIS' backlog of open investigations has increased to well over 2,000, and we had about 2,050 open investigations at the end of fiscal year 2011. These investigations include alleged violations involving animal welfare and horse protection issues, agricultural import and export rules, and quarantine rules, as well as unauthorized releases of genetically engineered organisms, violations of standards concerning accredited veterinarians, and unlicensed veterinary biological products.

Such a large backlog in open investigations has greatly impacted our enforcement process—primarily, the number of open investigations does not enable APHIS to swiftly address serious violations. In an attempt to streamline our investigation and enforcement process and ensure we pursue timely and appropriate sanctions for the most egregious violations, we are taking two interdependent actions: reducing the number of open investigations in the backlog and drastically decreasing the time it takes to resolve investigations. This effort is one of the six business process improvements the Secretary announced back in November that APHIS would be undertaking.

APHIS has determined that it has the capacity to process up to 1,000 investigations per year. However, the Agency first must focus on reducing the existing backlog and pursuing only those investigations (approximately 600 to 800) containing the most serious violations. To determine which investigations should be pursued and are of the highest priority, APHIS will be carefully weighing factors such as:

- each investigation's significance with respect to protecting plant and animal health and animal welfare,
- APHIS' ability to effectively pursue the alleged violation(s),
- the impact or seriousness of the alleged violation(s),
- the age of the alleged violation(s), and
- whether the investigation involves a person who has a history of not complying with APHIS regulatory requirements.

APHIS *Safeguarding American Agriculture*
APHIS is an agency of USDA's Marketing and Regulatory Programs
An Equal Opportunity Provider and Employer

Federal Relay Service
(Voice/TTY/ASCII/Spanish)
1-800-877-8339

Open Letter to Stakeholders:
Page 2

For those investigations we decide not to pursue and believe a warning may prevent future violations, we will issue official warning letters to close them out. These letters will clearly indicate that any further violations may result in more serious consequences such as civil penalties or criminal prosecution. We will also be working internally across all our programs and with the Department of Homeland Security's Customs and Border Protection to employ evaluation criteria—similar to those mentioned previously—so that we focus our resources on the most serious violations where we can achieve the most benefit and impact.

Reducing the backlog of open cases is just the first step—streamlining the enforcement process is equally important for maximizing efficiency and effectiveness. Current data indicate that it can take approximately 600 days, on average, to resolve an investigation and to pursue informal enforcement action, such as an official warning or stipulated monetary penalty. (Cases that are referred to the Department's Office of the General Counsel or Office of the Inspector General can take considerably longer.) Through our streamlining efforts, we expect to reduce the time it takes to resolve these investigations by approximately 40 percent, so that the average investigation is resolved within 365 days.

By taking actions like these, we are focusing on those mission priorities that matter most to our Agency and our stakeholders. We are committed to effective enforcement of our regulations, and we owe it to you, our stakeholders, to do so in the most efficient way. By targeting the most serious violations of our regulations, we are in turn addressing the biggest risk to agricultural health and the welfare of animals.

I look forward to updating you on the results of this important streamlining initiative in the coming months.

Sincerely,

Gregory L. Parham
Administrator

APHIS Factsheet

Investigative and Enforcement Services   January 2012

Questions and Answers: APHIS Enforcement Process Streamlining

The U.S. Department of Agriculture's (USDA) Animal and Plant Health Inspection Service (APHIS) is responsible for setting and enforcing regulations that protect the health and safety of American agriculture and natural resources. APHIS investigates and enforces penalties for violations involving animal welfare and horse protection issues; agricultural import and export rules, and quarantine rules. The Agency also targets unauthorized releases of genetically engineered organisms and enforces standards concerning accredited veterinarians and veterinary biological products. APHIS is very serious about taking enforcement action against those who jeopardize its mission by violating its regulations.

In recent years, however, the number of open enforcement investigations has increased to well over 2,000, a volume that has proven to be too large to enable APHIS to swiftly address and deter serious violations. Consequently, APHIS is in the process of streamlining its processes by reducing the number of open investigations in the backlog and drastically decreasing the time it takes to resolve an investigation. We believe that more timely enforcement action will better deter future violations of APHIS regulatory requirements. In addition, we realize that the length of time it currently takes to resolve investigations is frustrating for our stakeholders and not an effective or efficient use of our resources.

Q. Why does APHIS conduct investigations?
A. APHIS' Investigative and Enforcement Services (IES) unit investigates alleged violations of the statutes and regulations administered by Agency programs. These violations can have serious and costly impacts to American agriculture, the welfare of animals, and the public. Information gathered through investigations enables the Agency to pursue enforcement action against persons who do not comply with APHIS' regulatory requirements.

Q. How does the enforcement process work?
A. When APHIS program personnel discover apparent violations of our regulations, they may—depending on the seriousness of the issue—request that IES initiate a formal investigation, which includes gathering documentary and photographic evidence, interviewing witnesses, and other actions. After the investigation is complete, APHIS evaluates the evidence and determines whether to take one of a number of enforcement actions to address the alleged violations.

The action taken depends on the seriousness of the issues, the number of alleged violations, and other criteria. APHIS can decide to issue an official warning or a settlement agreement, which could include a monetary penalty or other sanction and is quicker and less costly than litigation. The Agency can also decide to pursue formal, legal prosecution through the administrative law process. Lastly, APHIS also refers some cases, such as those involving animal fighting or other serious matters, to USDA's Office of the Inspector General for possible criminal prosecution.

Q. How will APHIS improve the enforcement process?
A. There are two parts to this effort. First, APHIS is working to significantly reduce the current investigation backlog. By reducing the number of investigations in process at any given time, the Agency will be able to focus its resources on moving the investigations that involve the most serious violations through the enforcement process more expeditiously.

Second, APHIS is implementing improvements to the enforcement process identified during a successful Lean Six Sigma business process review and recent pilot test. These steps should improve internal communications and case management and thereby reduce the time it takes to process investigations.

Q. How many enforcement cases are currently pending?
A. At the end of fiscal year 2011, APHIS had approximately 2,050 investigated cases ongoing in the field or pending review and action in headquarters. Since then we have reduced that number to about 1,500. It is estimated that IES' maximum capacity for processing investigations is up to 1,000 cases per year.

Q. How will APHIS reduce the backlog of cases?
A. APHIS is working to identify, within the existing backlog of open investigations, those that are the highest priority for investigation and those that are

lower priority and should be withdrawn or closed out. To determine the highest priority cases, the Agency is using an analytical tool called Decision Lens that helps decision-makers weigh specific criteria. These criteria include: each investigation's significance with respect to protecting plant health, animal health, and the welfare of animals; APHIS' ability to effectively pursue the alleged violation(s); the age and potential impact of the alleged violation(s); and whether the investigation involves a person who has a history of not complying with APHIS regulatory requirements.

Q. When will APHIS start its backlog reduction efforts?
A. APHIS is already engaged in prioritizing cases.

Q. What will happen to the potential cases that are deemed lower priority? Will these cases simply be closed without further action?
A. As we sort through the investigations, we are identifying those that may not warrant potential judicial proceedings. Those investigations that we believe lack adequate supporting evidence will be closed. In general, for investigations that we believe contain substantiated violations, we will issue official warning letters. Although official warning letters do not include a monetary penalty, they are official enforcement actions and will be considered as part of a person's enforcement history if additional action is deemed necessary in the future.

We will also be using a compliance tool called "letters of information." Program personnel may send letters of information in response to non-egregious violations, with the aim of educating an individual on the correct way to remedy a lack of compliance with the Agency's regulations. Letters of information are an educational tool to help bring individuals into compliance with the law and build their relationship with our Agency. They will not be considered official enforcement action.

Q. Will APHIS add new cases while it deals with the backlog of cases? If so, how many new cases per year does APHIS intend to initiate?
A. APHIS will strive to maintain roughly 600-800 investigations in its system at any given time. We will also use the criteria developed to prioritize and evaluate current investigations to determine whether new investigations should be opened. This volume should enable us to pursue investigations effectively and meet our goals for issuing timely enforcement actions.

Q. How will it be determined in the future whether to open a case for investigation?
A. As APHIS officials are sorting through the current backlog of open investigations, they are collecting

information about the characteristics of those cases deemed to be of higher and lower priority. Based on this information, along with the factors mentioned above, each Agency program will then develop specific criteria to assist officials in determining whether to refer or accept new potential cases for investigation.

Q. Does this new approach mean that APHIS will be less aggressive in its enforcement efforts?
A. Absolutely not. APHIS is better utilizing resources currently available to meet its regulatory mission. By prioritizing potential enforcement investigations, the Agency can ensure that more serious violations receive the attention necessary to bring about justice quicker. Faster processing of investigations should also stop further violations from occurring while waiting for a lengthy investigative process to conclude.

Q. What other steps is APHIS taking to streamline the enforcement process?
A. The process streamlining effort includes, among other things: creating templates to standardize communication and reduce errors; pursuing action on the most serious and best substantiated violations in any given investigation rather than delaying to collect evidence to support additional violations; and taking a more national, rather than regional or local, approach to enforcement and policy decisions. These changes will improve investigation management, internal communication, and decision-making.

Q. How will these efforts improve the time it takes to process a case?
A. At present, it takes an average of about 600 days to resolve an investigation of alleged violations and to pursue informal enforcement action, such as an official warning or stipulated monetary penalty. (Cases that are referred to the Department's Office of the General Counsel or Office of the Inspector General can take considerably longer.) Through our streamlining efforts, we expect to reduce the average time it takes to resolve an investigation to 365 days. This would amount to a time savings of about approximately 40 percent.

Q. Where does the penalty money go when fines are paid? Will APHIS use this to increase the investigator workforce?
A. Penalties paid in connection with alleged violations are paid to the general fund of the U.S. Treasury, like penalties paid in connection with violations of nearly all Federal statutes. APHIS, like other Federal agencies, is not authorized to keep or utilize any portion of the penalties assessed.

USDA is an equal opportunity provider, employer and lender. To file a complaint of discrimination, write: USDA, Director, Office of Civil Rights, 1400 Independence Ave., SW, Washington, DC 20250-9410 or call (800) 795-3272 (voice), or (202) 720-6382 (TDD).

ONLINE RESOURCES*

Animal Welfare Act, 7 U.S.C. § 2131 et seq.:

http://www.aphis.usda.gov/animal_welfare/downloads/awa/awa.pdf

Note: The most current version of United States Code is available at http://uscode.house.gov

Animal Welfare Act and Animal Welfare Regulations, (November 2013):

http://www.aphis.usda.gov/animal_welfare/downloads/Animal%20Care%20Blu e%20Book%20-%202013%20-%20FINAL.pdf

Note: The most current version of the Code of Federal Regulations is available at: http://www.ecfr.gov

Animal Care Policy Manual (March 7, 2014):

Note: The link for this version is currently unavailable. Please see the APHIS Stakeholder Registry notice updating Policy 3, available at: http://content.govdelivery.com/accounts/USDAAPHIS/bulletins/aafd1c.   The original Animal Care Resource Guide Policies (March 25, 2011) is available at: http://www.aphis.usda.gov/animal_welfare/downloads/Animal%20Care%20Poli cy%20Manual.pdf

***Animal Welfare Inspection Guide* (September 2013):**

http://www.aphis.usda.gov/animal_welfare/downloads/Animal%20Care%20Ins pection%20Guide.pdf

USDA, APHIS: http://www.aphis.usda.gov/wps/portal/aphis/home/

USDA, APHIS, Animal Care:

http://www.aphis.usda.gov/wps/portal/aphis/ourfocus/animalwelfare

USDA, APHIS, Investigative and Enforcement Services:

http://www.aphis.usda.gov/wps/portal/aphis/resources/enforcement-actions

Animal Welfare Information Center: http://awic.nal.usda.gov/

* The United States Department of Agriculture Animal and Plant Health Inspection Service authorizes the use of links for information available on its website.

ABOUT THE AUTHOR

James F. Gesualdi has dedicated himself to his work on legal, regulatory and strategic matters regarding animal welfare and wildlife conservation. He works extensively with the U.S. Animal Welfare Act and champions ways to improve its administration and enforcement, as well as engaging in consensus building on related policy matters.

Gesualdi's leadership experience includes serving as chair of the New York State Bar Association Committee on Animals and the Law; founding co-chair of the Suffolk County Bar Association Animal Law Committee; vice chair of the American Bar Association Young Lawyers Division Animal Protection Committee; and as a vice chair of the American Bar Association Tort Trial and Insurance Practice Section Animal Law Committee. He has also been a member of the Section of Administrative Law and Regulatory Practice. He has served as special professor of law at Hofstra University School of Law, where he has taught Animal Law. He has also served on the faculty of the Association of Zoos and Aquariums' "Zoo School" for zoological professionals, where he taught courses on ethical considerations relating to animals.

He was special counsel to the marine mammal community's Working Group on the Reintroduction of Marine Mammals to the Wild and participated in the U.S. Department of Agriculture Animal Plant and Health Inspection Service's Marine Mammal Negotiated Rulemaking, completing a voluminous "Analysis and Commentary" on this subject.

He earned his B.A. degree from St. Lawrence University where he graduated magna cum laude, Phi Beta Kappa, with highest honors in Government; his M.A. in Political Science (Public Affairs) from the State University of New York at Stony Brook; and his J.D. degree from the Hofstra University School of Law from which he graduated with Distinction and where he served as a Notes and Comments Editor of the Law Review. His work has been profiled in the *American Bar Association Journal*, the *New York Times*, the *New York Law Journal*, *Newsday*, *Long Island Business News* and in Yolanda Eisenstein's *Careers in Animal Law*.

Connecting with
EXCELLENCE BEYOND COMPLIANCE

To learn more about incorporating EXCELLENCE BEYOND COMPLIANCE into your organization through seminars and training opportunities, please email us at:

info@excellencebeyondcompliance.com

Additionally, whether you are a professional or volunteer dedicated to your work with animals, a visitor at a zoological organization, or someone committed to enhancing animal welfare or making a difference through the Animal Welfare Act, your thoughts are welcome. Please email us at the above address. We would also welcome mention of outstanding individuals and organizations committed to excellence in enhancing animal welfare.

Laws, regulations and interpretations change constantly. Check the agency webpages noted in the Online Resources section of this book for current information. For updates to EXCELLENCE BEYOND COMPLIANCE, please visit:

http://excellencebeyondcompliance.com/

Thank you!

Not the maker of plans and promises, but rather the one who offers faithful service in small matters. This is the person who is most likely to achieve what is good and lasting.

Johann Wolfgang von Goethe